THE SCOUT LEADER'S HANDBOOK

THE SCOUT LEADER'S HANDBOOK

The official Handbook of
The Scout Association

Published by
The Scout Association,
25 Buckingham Palace Road,
London SW1W 0PY.

SBN 85165 060 0.

First Edition.
July 1967.

Fifth printing.
March 1974.

Printed in Great Britain by
Kent Paper Company Ltd.

CONTENTS

FOREWORD

No book, however good, can be expected to supply all the answers and this Handbook is no exception. Be this as it may, it is hoped that within its pages there will be found sufficient information and knowledge to enable the average Scout Leader to become an above average Leader and the good Leader an even better one.

We have endeavoured to present this Handbook in the light of the many changes that have taken place in the Scout Movement. It is realised, however, that with the advantages of practical experience of the training scheme it may become necessary to effect further minor changes in detail but it is not anticipated that there will be any major alterations for some years. Therefore, this Handbook should become a text book for Leaders of the Scout Section and, as such, it is hoped that it will prove of constructive and practical value to the new Leader as well as to those who have served in this capacity for some time.

The Boy and Young Man whom this Handbook seeks to serve through Scouting is the hub of the Movement and the leadership that he is given is of vital importance. Youth of the present day and tomorrow requires the leadership of those who, in addition to experience and dedication, possess a deep knowledge of their subject. This Handbook aspires to provide some of this knowledge in the hope that the Scout Section will derive effective, practical and lasting benefit from its pages.

We thank all the writers who out of their considerable knowledge and experience have contributed to this Handbook.

ACKNOWLEDGEMENTS

We acknowledge, with gratitude, all who have helped with the production of this book and particularly those photographers who have so kindly permitted us to use their photographs, i.e. Neil D. Davis, P. W. Hand, R. B. Herbert, Roger B. Keeney, Jim Laurence, Norman A. Rowe, Colin A. Wood and the Headquarters Publicity Department.

Chapter 1

WHAT IS THE SCOUT MOVEMENT?

This is a simple question which, in the end, needs a complex answer. But one can begin simply and factually: it is a uniformed Movement for boys and young men, known as The Scout Association, and it arose, more or less spontaneously, from the publicising and publishing of his ideas, notably in a book called *Scouting for Boys*, by a soldier-hero of his day, Robert Stephenson Smythe Baden-Powell, who had shown more than a flash of genius in transferring Scouting from the army to the life of boys. The name Baden-Powell became, because of his resourceful defence of Mafeking at the turn of the century, a household word: because of this his somewhat novel ideas of how boys might wish to spend their leisure were the more quickly propagated and the more easily accepted. Scouting spread like a flame in stubble, which perhaps it was. Thousands of boys, and especially the non-attached who had found themselves unattracted by such Youth Movements as existed, here in Scouting found something that met their needs. Boys hurriedly tied scarves round their necks, found broomsticks and looked around for men to lead them; and men, inspired by that same book, looked for boys to lead.

"I suppose every British boy wants to help his country in

some way or other" ran the famous sentence, but this does not apply only to British boys. The writer, the day he wrote this in 1966, received a letter from a young Indian Scout from Darjeeling which ended: "It is fun being a Scout and helping my country and helping people." All over the world, boys were asking insistently: "How do we become Scouts?" and very soon, too, younger brothers were knocking at the Troop door, and B.-P. had to invent (with the help of Rudyard Kipling's *Jungle Stories*) Wolf Cubs, now known as Cub Scouts.

Before many months were out, Scout Troops were organised into Districts and Counties, and the first edition of *Policy, Organisation and Rules* had, in 1911, appeared. Scouts were attending rallies showing the world, and one another, their enthusiastic existence. In 1911, too, they took on what was to be one of their major assignments (and still is) — assistance on a Royal occasion, when they were on duty at the Coronation. Since then they have served on many more occasions at Royal weddings, Coronations, Royal garden parties; at Olympic and Commonwealth Games, too. What Wells called 'a new sort of boy' who used his leisure adventurously but sensibly became, with his good turn (which became a part of English speech as Bob-a-Job did later), and his typical hat, a part of the British scene. Thousands upon thousands of boyhoods were better and happier because of the Scouts. This is not the place (nor is there the space) to go into the detailed history of sixty years of the Movement: even its milestones would occupy pages! For that you should turn to the official history, *B-P's Scouts* (Collins) or *Two Lives of a Hero* (Heinemann, £3.50), both of which you will find of the greatest interest. (Your local library will probably have copies.)

The aim of the Movement in its current statement is "to encourage the physical, mental and spiritual developments of young people so that they may take a constructive place in society." The method of achieving the Association's aim is "by providing an enjoyable and attractive scheme of progressive training, based on the Scout Law and Promise and guided by adult leadership."

The Scout Movement considers its birthday to be a camp held on Brownsea Island in Poole Harbour in August, 1907;

at least this emphasises an essential fact that, although the details of its training change in no particularly significant ways from year to year, Scouting remains essentially an out-of-doors Movement. Inevitably our climate and a boy's commitments of home and school life mean that much of his Scout training takes place indoors, but this in no way alters the fact that the Scouting method is based on camping and life under the open skies. B.-P., as he became affectionately known, believed that there were many boys who dreamed of being pioneers and explorers who, given the chance, would enjoy learning the skills needed by such men and that as a consequence both they and their country would be better for it. His own boyhood and his experience of the boys of Mafeking convinced him (rightly) that boys could lead boys, and that in the first half of their 'teens anyway liked to belong to a 'gang'—a closely knit community eager for excitement and adventure which an increasingly urban environment was subtracting from their lives.

Scouting is not for every boy: it is for the boy who is willing to make an effort to live up to a code of behaviour and to undertake certain obligations. He is expected to attend regularly meetings of his Patrol (which is what the 'gang' of six or seven boys is called), the weekly meetings of the Troop, which is an assembly of three, four, five or more Patrols, and summer camps and other camps as are included in the Troop's programme. He will normally do this because to enjoy outdoor activities and camping and the like is his reason for remaining "in the Scouts."

Perhaps in trying to answer our simple question it is time to ask what the boy who joins expects from the Movement? We would suggest six things:

(1) He wants action. He wants to *do* things. When the original Scouts opened their copies of *Scouting for Boys* they found it was full of things they could *do* — signal, tie knots, build bridges, put up a tent, light a fire, cook a meal. A scout was a man of action; so was a Scout!

(2) Even more, he wants *adventurous action*. Of course, adventure is a many-coloured thing and what is adventure to an eleven-year-old may have become a bore to a sixteen-year-old. But it is basic that Scouting that doesn't provide

high-spirited adventure — and plenty of it, and regularly — hasn't begun to be Scouting: whoever called Scouting 'legalised mischief' was on the right trail! It is also basic that the adventure must progress from the simple (for example) thrill of sleeping under canvas for the first time or cooking one's own breakfast over the camp-fire one has successfully lit (and this can all be really thrilling for an eleven-year-old), to the realistic challenges of deep cave or rock face or turbulent river which the older boy or the young man demands.

(3) He needs *achievement* (all boys do: what is delinquency but achievement that has taken the wrong turning?). It is not enough to learn new skills: he must be seen to have learnt such skills, which is why a badge system has been such an integral part of Scouting from its first beginnings.

B.-P. took the dreams of the boy of that day and turned them into reality. It has never been better expressed than in a book published some years ago called *The Gardens of Paradise Alley*. The author, Bernard Wetherall, recalling his London boyhood, writes of the early years of Scouting and of a certain shop window he and his pals observed: "In the window were two tailor's dummies dressed in full Scout's uniform, sitting over what was supposed to be a camp-fire. From three Scouts' staffs hung a cauldron. All around them were arranged . . . knives, axes, belts, whistles . . . on the floor as well as on the walls . . . hats, shirts, lanyards, mess tins complete with a frying pan with a handle that folded inside — bowie knives in leather cases and photographs of Baden-Powell. We just stood and gazed at all these things for a long, long, time. Every article displayed touched a cord within us. For years our minds had dwelt in an atmosphere where all these things were the essentials of the life we dreamed about."

The dreams alter but not greatly, and the boy who saw himself yesterday tracking through the African bush or with Kim on the Great Trunk Road, today sees himself as an astronaut or deep sea diver, but the cipher of a boy's dreams can be translated clearly as just a longing to be self-reliant and self-independent and to stand on his own feet and to know what to do when the time comes. So his training, his achievement, must be progressive.

(4) He needs a sense of *belonging*. 'There are no strangers

here' should be written above every Scout Headquarters. A Scout's Troop should be a 'home from home.' A distinguished public figure of our own day has written in his autobiography: "Scouting provided the other life which often supplanted school and even home life in my mind." "I know," wrote a mother to Scout Headquarters not long ago, "how much Scouting has meant and does mean to our son and we appreciate all it has done to help him find a true sense of value and to make him a whole person." Another mother wrote: "I would like to say that although now only 14 years old, Scouting has played a major part in my son's young life. He *lives* for Scouting." A Scout feels that in the Movement he has joined he will receive friendship and understanding; and he will. Perhaps this all came out of the "secret society" ethos of the early days — the left handshake, the motto, the solemn promise; quite early it was fostered by international gatherings; the phrase 'Scout Brotherhood' was widely used. A Scout has friends everywhere and they are called Scouts, too.

(5) He needs *fun*! A boy doesn't come to Scouting (or to any other Movement) to be made a good citizen or a more religious person: he will accept these as by-products, but he becomes a Scout because he hopes to enjoy himself.

(6) A chance for *service* — believe it or not! Inside every boy is an idealist trying to get out — and it was part of B.-P.'s genius to recognise this. Other men no doubt could have and would have devised a programme for youth to include the call of the wild and the skills of the open air man, but what other man would have known that it would appeal to most boys if accompanied by a promise to take, a law to live up to, and a continuing demand on his compassion — for this, in effect, was what the good turn amounted to? So the idea of service to others is as essential to the Scouting ethos as adventure, or progressive achievement, or friendship or fun.

If a Scout enters a Troop — a worthwhile Troop, of course, for it would be idle to pretend that all are of the highest standard — where he has been properly trained and attained the various Standards which mark his progress, he will be skilled and experienced in many ways. He will know how to camp, i.e. how to pack a rucsac, put up a tent, cook a meal either with utensils or without; he will know how to make himself comfortable in field or forest and, if no tent is available, will be able to erect a shelter for the night. He will know a fair amount of first-aid, be able to deal with minor injuries or how to apply oral resuscitation. He will be able to set, read and use a map and how to use an axe and look after it; he will know the correct knots to use in camp or on a boat and know what precautions are necessary on any worthwhile activity. He will know something about the weather and something about the countryside and something about other matters not always thought of perhaps as strictly Scouting. He will know that when emergencies occur — fire, drowning and the like — he must be prepared to act on his knowledge. He will be able to build a bridge and log-up timber. All this is Scouting. He will have tried, looking at the problem from different viewpoints as he grew taller from eleven to sixteen, to live up to the Scout Law. He will have grown in consciousness of the needs of others, and will have tried to help them whenever it was possible for him to do so within the limits of his boyhood's years: and so in the best of all ways, he will have helped himself. This is Scouting, too.

We have said "All over the world boys were asking 'How can we become Scouts?'," and they are asking the question — where they are allowed to ask it — insistently still. Today there are some eleven million active members of the Movement of all ages in nearly ninety countries. (Nine countries, alas, once happy with their Scouts, no longer possess any, as their present Governments do not tolerate free institutions.)

When a Scout is enrolled he is often, indeed usually, welcomed into "the World-Wide Brotherhood of Scouts." To keep the many different parts of this brotherhood in friendship and understanding together, a slight but important control was devised in 1920. It has three constituent parts: (a) A Conference, which meets every two years, to strengthen the bonds between the Scouting countries, each of which, no matter what its size, sends six delegates and has six votes! (b) A World Committee which consists of twelve different members of twelve different countries, one-third of the members retiring each year and no one person being permitted to serve for more than six consecutive years. It is important to note that the

Committee members represent the Conference and act for it — they do not represent the countries from which they come. (c) A bureau, or office which carries out the policy laid down by the Conference and the Committee. (It is, after being in London and Ottawa, now situated in Geneva.)

The Conference has two important tasks; first, it has to decide which invitation shall be accepted from countries offering to be hosts at world gatherings such as Jamborees; secondly, it has to elect members to the World Committee. Amongst the duties of this Committee should be mentioned that of considering applications for membership of the Conference from countries that wish to be registered, countries where Scouting has been established for the first time or others (former members) who, after a period of suppression by autocratic governments, are eager to rejoin their old comrades.

Before an Association can be registered, the Committee must be satisfied that the organisation of the Movement there is in complete accord with the principles and methods laid down by B.-P. and based on a Promise and Law. The Conference is a conference of adult Scouts, men of different traditions, creeds, tongues, colours, but all alike in this: they believe in Scouting and are dedicated to serving its cause, as men have always been since that August week of 1907. For without men, the boys could not be very adequate Scouts, as they soon discovered. Parents and policemen and parsons all in their varying ways had to be placated and pleased: usually, as understanding of Scouting grew, they were eager, it seemed, to help. Scoutmasters were needed to lead and advise and teach the Patrol Leaders so that they in their turn could lead, advise and teach their Scouts; instructors were needed to instruct and Badge Examiners to examine. Men of standing were required to head up Districts and Counties as Commissioners. Laymen were needed as Secretaries and Treasurers. The men always came, sometimes to their surprise; and it must be said, just as in the lives of many Scouts the Movement is a kind of glory shining, so it is in the lives of many men who have found themselves immeasurably enriched by the comradeship and the adventure and most of all by the trust and affection of the boys with the arrow-head badge. But there have never been enough adult leaders: there never will be, for the more

Leaders the Movement has, the more efficient, virile and ambitious it will become and the more boys it will attract. There are always boys waiting. There are always men needed.

Chapter 2

FUNDAMENTALS

THE SPIRIT OF SCOUTING

We have seen that Scouting is a Movement for boys, with its emphasis on camping, the outdoors and all those activities and pursuits which are attractive to boys, but so are many other Youth Organisations. Scouting, however, is different from the others in one thing, not only different but unique. What makes it so is sometimes called the 'ethos' of Scouting. This is a Greek word which means the spirit, and it is that which this chapter is all about. The essence of this spirit is to be found in the Promise and the Law. This is important for you, the Leader, because the many boys who enter our Movement will be attracted by the outdoor life, the camping, but hardly the spirit as such. It will be your job to get this over to the boys, so you should know something of what it is all about.

THE PROMISE

ON MY HONOUR I PROMISE
THAT I WILL DO MY BEST
TO DO MY DUTY TO GOD AND TO THE QUEEN,
TO HELP OTHER PEOPLE
AND TO KEEP THE SCOUT LAW.

You, and all your boys, are making *of your own free will* a promise or oath to do your best to serve God, your country and your neighbour . . . and the signposts showing you what such service implies are laid down in the Law.

Now let us look at this in more detail. First of all, it is voluntary. If there was any compulsion brought to bear, then that Promise could have no moral force at all. You have *chosen* to bind yourself to it, and it is this responsibility which carries the power.

Secondly, the Promise says 'On my honour.' B.-P. throughout his life emphasised the development of a sense of honour in a boy. Now you cannot inject a sense of honour into a boy like some drug, but you *can* treat him as a responsible being, by trusting him 'on his honour,' and showing that such trust is based on his having taken a solemn oath 'on his honour.'

Thirdly, the Promise says 'I will do my best.' This recognizes that people of 11, 16 or 60 are human beings with the possibility of all the human failings. If this phrase were not put into the Promise, then the latter becomes too much of a challenge. With these words inserted it is brought down to a level when all of us, whether we be newly invested Recruit, or Scouter of 20 years service, can feel that if he *is* doing his best, then he is true to his first undertaking.

DUTY TO GOD

This is a fundamental obligation laid upon all invested members of our Movement . . . yes, including, or especially, you. The religious faith to which a Scout belongs is fully safeguarded: he is expected and encouraged to fulfil his church duties (and you will do the encouraging). Those Scouts who do not belong to churches are to be brought into touch with religious ideas, by the prayers said at Troop meetings, by Scouts' Own services, but chiefly by your example, how *you* put duty to God into practice. (See chapters 3 and 4, which have more to say about this part of the Promise.)

DUTY TO THE QUEEN

Every Scout is expected to be loyal to his own country, and to serve it to the best of his ability, according to his opportunities, and this is expressed in the Promise in the form of duty to the Queen as the titular head of our land. This does not mean a slavish conformity to any particular political doctrine, for our training in citizenship has nothing to do with political practice. The facts of our society should be presented so that each of our members comes to his own conclusions. There must, however, be a recognition that we must conform to certain things for our properly organised society to continue to exist. If a law is considered bad, then it should not be broken, but efforts made to get it changed within the proper legal framework.

DUTY TO ONE'S NEIGHBOUR

Every Scout is expected to put this positively into practice. This is worked out in the Law, but there are two further points you should note.

First of all, the Scout motto is 'Be Prepared.' This is a constant reminder to every Scout that his Promise and Law are real things. In his training a Scout prepares himself to be useful to others. He learns to look after himself, and to keep a cool head in emergencies so that he can look after others.

Secondly, there is what is often called the 'Scout Grin.' This is just as much an essential element in the spirit of Scouting and in the Law. B.-P. often reminded people about cheerfulness. He also said that in the Movement we should not take ourselves 'too damn seriously.' This is another important aspect of helping others. What a morale booster it is to be faced by a cheerful, smiling face! Here is truly a way to help others by becoming the epitome of cheerfulness. You should always remember that Scouting is a game and that, as B.-P. said, if Scouting loses its laughter then it will lose its appeal and success.

THE LAW

The Scout Law sets down in plain language the code of conduct which is the basis of good citizenship. It puts before the boy in POSITIVE, not negative, terms such virtues and duties as loyalty, friendliness, courtesy, courage and respect. Practical ways of making these real should be provided in the life of the Troop, as we shall see (here's where *you* come in again). The beginning of this is to be found in the daily Good Turn, which inculcates the habit of thoughtfulness for others. The boys should know the Law thoroughly. Let us start with the order in which they come. Since the beginning of Scouting, one of the aids used to remember things of importance, has been the rhyming couplet. Here is one to help with the Laws and the order in which they come:

Trusty, loyal, friends and brothers,
Courageous, careful, respect for others.

1. A Scout is to be trusted

Right at the start, once again, is emphasised that if a boy has taken the Scout Promise he can be trusted . . . he *is* responsible, and you must at every available opportunity show this in your own living. Equally you can show that you expect a similar response from the boy himself. You expect that he will not break his honour, he will not tell lies, he will endeavour to put into practice his duty to God, he will help other people.

2. A Scout is loyal

The loyalty to country defined in the Promise is now extended. A Scout is expected to be loyal to all with whom he is involved in society. At its most immediate level this means his Patrol Leader, those with him in Patrol and Troop; to his parents, to his Scouters, to his school, and to his friends. Later, as he matures, this list will widen. When he accepts employment, he should accord this loyalty to his employer. Such organisations as his Church and Youth Club will deserve the same measure of loyalty. This involves a Scout sticking to those people and things to which he has committed himself, in bad times and good, in refusing to listen to people who talk badly of them or slander them in any way. It is so easy to talk or think badly of somebody or to put the worst interpretation on the words and actions of somebody else. This a loyal Scout will not do. You, as the Leader, will set an example in this; you will not countenance the sly innuendo or caustic statement.

3. A Scout is friendly and considerate

The Promise lays down that a Scout should help other people, and this law amplifies what such helpfulness entails.

A Scout is friendly in that he accepts a person as he finds him, and accepts him cheerfully, so that the person can *see* that he is accepted. He is considerate in that he takes account of people's feelings, he is polite in his everyday meetings with people. He realizes that animals and birds are God's creatures and does not treat them cruelly. He does not look for any reward for being helpful, polite or courteous and indeed he will not accept such rewards if they are offered. You, as Leader, will do the same, not only in individual action, but for the Troop as a whole. In what ways? You will reply promptly to letters, attend Scouting meetings, participate in other activities. This is setting the example in a practical way which will not be lost on your boys.

4. A Scout is a brother to all Scouts

Here is embodied the *particular* relationship between Scouts all over the world, who have taken the Scout Promise, and we welcome with the left handshake everybody who is a member of the Brotherhood. A Scout meets a fellow Scout, and knowing he has taken the same or similar Promise treats him as a brother, if necessary helps him, makes him his friend, and this no matter whether that Scout is of different religion, different colour, whether he is rich or poor. To you as Leader falls much in this field too, not only by encouraging the international aspects of Scouting, helping Scout visitors to this country and the like, but also at Troop level. Have you any favourites in the Troop? If so, it makes mockery of this law. Do you hesitate to take a boy in, perhaps because he is handicapped, perhaps because he is a rare handful? This law for you may come much nearer home in its impact than any wonderful ideals of international brotherhood. (See chapter 16 — "International Scouting.")

5. A Scout has courage in all difficulties

This life has its ups and downs . . . the rough and the smooth; and a Scout should be trained to be prepared for both. This does not only mean that a Scout is able to 'grin and bear it,' it is a lot more than that. If adverse circumstances come about then a Scout should square his shoulders and face up to those difficulties. There is an old saying 'God helps those who help themselves,' and this law underlies that. A Scout should not complain when things are not going right; he should not grumble when put out. He may be able to put on a cheerful grin to the outside world, but if he cannot, then he should at least show that he is ready to face adversity and *do* something about it. You, also, must be ready to show that when things go wrong, whether in the Troop or outside, you are prepared to have a go at sorting them out, and if things still do not work out, that you will not throw in the sponge and moan or complain.

6. A Scout makes good use of his time and is careful of possessions and property

Today our highly complex society is characterised by continual rush and bustle and it is essential that a person should be able to fit himself into this pattern. So a Scout will get himself organised. He will, in fact, organise himself so that he is able to play a fruitful role within society. If he is at school, a Scout will sort out his time so that he can do his homework properly, attend his Troop or Patrol meeting, fulfil his religious obligations by going to church. Later if he is working he will husband his resources to make the best use of them, his own talents and also the money he earns. But not only this, he will take care of what he has; he will not waste anything, and will equally care for what is his as a member of society — that is, what is public property. He will not deface seats in public parks; he will not leave litter. As a responsible Scout those things which belong to other people he will treasure, as he would expect his own possessions to be treasured by others. You will see that this is being carried out in your Troop. If, for instance, you meet in a school, you will take care of school property. If you meet in a church hall you will ensure that the chairs are carefully stacked, the floor left clean.

7. A Scout has respect for himself and for others

There are two aspects of this. First, because God has given him a body, a mind and a spirit, then a Scout should have respect for all three within himself. He should not abuse his body by over-indulgence or misuse, his mind should be used properly, so that with his spirit he becomes a personality worthy of his Maker. Secondly, a Scout should realise that other people are the same as he in this way, so that he has an equal respect for their bodies, their minds. This means no misuse of their bodies, no wrong indoctrination of their minds. Does this seem heavy stuff to you, Leader? Well, it is and rightly so, because this is what should follow in our daily lives from our religious beliefs and practices. Not easy to put over to your boys? Certainly it is not. Important things never are easy. The casual swear word, the smutty joke, this is the beginning of the falling away from this law. You must be prepared to face up to the difficulties and temptations your boys meet up with as regards this sort of thing and, let's face it, the most likely aspect is with regard to sex. This may not be the pattern with a boy in his early days in the Troop. Here an emphasis on health in body and mind is usually sufficient. As time passes, however, if you are a Leader who really leads, boys will come to you about emotional problems and those concerning sex. Don't reject them! Don't be embarrassed! Equally, do not worry if your answers seem inadequate. If you are sincere in what you say, however awkwardly expressed, they *will* get over.

THE LEADER IN ACTION

It is important to *do* something positive about this fundamental basis of our Scouting, and in particular duty to God.

First and foremost, without doubt you must use your Patrol Leaders' Council — after all, the Patrol System is supposed to be the basic method in our work, and it should be used in this sphere, perhaps more than any other. B.-P. emphasised that the Council should be "the guardian of the honour of the Troop," and this should obviously include things spiritual.

Secondly, you can use *all* Scouting activities — woodcraft, nature and the rest —as a lead to the understanding of the wonders of God as Creator. In addition, all activities should be specifically related to the Promise and Law. You should point out, for example, that a violation of the Country Code is contrary to the Scout Law. Such relationships should be progressive. Your 11-year-old is far more ready to accept this in "black and white" terms, than the 15-year-old with his doubts and lack of conviction. In that case, you should try to explain logically to him the whys and wherefores of the link between any one activity and his Promise.

Thirdly, you should be available and ready to discuss with your Scouts their spiritual problems. Some people may say . . . "Well, what about the local vicar? That's *his* province." It is, but you are the Leader, and they are *your* boys . . . your boys who will look naturally to *you*, and will not be over-worried if you have not got all the answers "off pat." They may even think you are trying your best, and that has got them right back to the Promise.

Fourthly, and really following from the last attitude, your recruitment policy with regard to adults should be aimed at bringing in to help those people for whom the boys have a respect by virtue of their knowledge of their job . . . men who are genuinely religious in the best sense, and who can, therefore, by their actions and presence evoke a response from the boys. Is it not a fact that people will sometimes listen to Adam Faith or David Shepherd talking about their faith with a greater attention than they would to the local minister or priest? We don't all have Adam Faiths living in the district, but I am sure there are some of similar stature to be found.

Fifthly, you should use the opportunity to have prayers at Troop Meetings. In Open Groups all prayers and, indeed, services must be voluntary, but the *opportunity* for prayer should be provided. Now, obviously the choice of prayers must be suited to the ages of the boys and appropriate to the occasion. But why not leave the choice to the boys? And why not sometimes have the boys make up the prayers for them-selves? It is a good Patrol activity and the results should be understood by the boys and acceptable to them.

Sixthly, there is the Scouts' Own Service. Like all corporate prayer of the right sort this can be a "bridge between spiritual ignorance and ultimate conviction." Such a service should include the ingredients of Hymns, Prayers, Reading, Scout Law and Yarn or Talk. But it is the blend that is important. Do not put all your prayers in one place; split them up. A boy can only absorb a little at a time, and in any case it will have a greater impact in this way. Do not have Hymns if only a few boys are present. Take the Readings from a modern trans lation of the Bible. Yarns should, on the whole, be short and to the point, and indeed may be superseded by a straight talk if only older boys are present. In any case such yarns or talks should never exceed ten minutes . . . and remember the shorter the talk the harder and longer is the preparation required.

Having listed all these points, one further note should be made, and heavily underlined. You should not make all this a sort of medicine which a boy has to swallow as one of the requirements of being in Scouting. The boy should *enjoy* his religion and his relationship with God, as he enjoys any other aspect of his Scouting. This is really that Scout Grin again in our spiritual life — Yes! *our* spiritual life, for if everything mentioned above is what you should do, it is even more important what *we* should *be*.

There are many qualities it is desirable for us to possess, but three of these are very necessary. First of all faithful; that is, full of faith, for the stronger our faith, the more it will rub off on our boys. Much more will be caught than taught. We should also strengthen our toleration. We must acknowledge that we do not hold a monopoly of truth, and show that fact in our lives. But such toleration must not be the *tolerance* of things that are not quite right. It should not be the tolerance of trying to please all the people all of the time. In fact, if necessary, we must not be afraid to be militant, yes militant against those things which will be wrong for our boys. A man is free to be an atheist or an agnostic, but dare we allow him to indoctrinate our boys as a Leader in the Movement? No! It would be contrary to Law 7, and we must be militant and state firmly that our fundamentals are of no use whatsoever if they do not include Duty to God. Faith, toleration, militancy, these are only three qualities . . . there are many more, most of which are summed up in a well-known and ancient prayer . . .

> "Be of good courage, hold fast to that which is good, render to no man evil for evil, strengthen the faint hearted, support the weak, help the afflicted, honour all men, love and serve the Lord . . . "

. . . and with all these we should enjoy it . . . and it should show!

Chapter 3

THE SCOUT

In the previous two chapters we have attempted to explain something about the Scout Movement and its fundamentals. Now we come to the most important factor in the whole set-up — the Scout, or the boy himself. Without him everything else would be pointless, and it has always been an important feature of this "game" to remember its most vital single factor, without which Scouting would never have come into being.

It follows, therefore, that those who are entrusted with the job of legislating and of making the rules and regulations for Scouting should never, at any time, lose sight of its main objective which is: "The aim of the Association is to encourage the physical, mental and spiritual development of young people so that they may take a constructive place in society."

In this overall aim the Scout section has a difficult job to perform, for it has to deal with the 11-to-16-year-old during his transition from boyhood to adolescence or mid-adolescence. In doing this it must seek to satisfy the aspirations and needs of both.

The characteristics of the boy of 11 are very different from those of the 16-year-old and this is of the greatest importance when considering the Scout section. The average boy during this five-year period passes through a major physiological and psychological change. It is established that boys mature physically at an earlier age than a few decades ago, and although it is not clear whether they mature emotionally any earlier, it is certain that they are more sophisticated at an earlier age than were their parents.

At 11 years the boy is highly imaginative and active. He wants to play at adventure through games and finds real adventure in new experiences such as camping and simple Scout activities; he wants to make personal progress and acquire new skills quickly; he enjoys the status of being an accepted member of a "gang" on the whole older than himself and admires the *savoir faire* of those a few years older than himself. He accepts established codes and practices without giving them much thought, has little or no spontaneous desire to serve others and is generally not interested in girls. It ought to be remembered, though, that although boys of this age are inevitably handicapped by their lack of knowledge and experience of the adult world they have the benefit of seeing everything for the first time with clear eyes. The direct, practical and sincere outlook of childhood is still with them and has not been "sicklied o'er by the pale cast of thought" or overlaid by self-deceptions and false values. This gives them a kind of wisdom which is a most precious attribute of youth, especially at this stage of their lives.

The boy of 11 to 13 is a hero worshipper. More is said about this in the next chapter but here it is sufficient to mention that he responds willingly to leadership and has a great trust in those who teach and guide him. He is intensely loyal to them. In short, he takes what is given him and asks few questions in return and responds to the leadership and example of the Scout Leader — to his manliness — for he sees here the image of what he himself would like to become. All this brings great responsibility to the Leader, for the boy must not be let down, his faith and trust must not be impaired.

Around 14 to 16 years the boy undergoes considerable change. He is quite rightly now fiercely striving to outgrow his childish traits and, above all, his need to be dependent on adults. This is a perfectly natural development for if it did not occur he would remain immature and dependent on others. We should recognise, though, that it is this very thing which often tends to cause so much disruption of the relationships between him and his parents and in many cases with his teachers and all forms of authority. Other manifestations may well include phases of negativism and emotional withdrawal from adults and activities associated with them. There are other factors, too. Our boy/youth is so eager to participate in all the exciting new fields of experience and adventure that are opening up for him in modern times and, as a consequence of all this excitement, he often tends to feel completely lost and overwhelmed. The resultant insecurity, coupled with his demand for independence, often makes him unwilling to accept the help and guidance of his parents or, indeed, any adult. He is afraid to be thought childish or inadequate by grown-ups and lives in terror of the criticism of his contemporaries. Thus he is faced by the constant need to prove himself to himself and to others. Is it any wonder that he has problems?

We find other changes, too. He is now no longer interested in merely playing imaginative games but enjoys taking a leading part in organising them; he finds real adventure in testing himself in physically and mentally challenging situations; he wants to prove himself by continuing to make personal progress; he enjoys the status of being looked up to by younger boys and wants to be treated as an equal by adults, but is at times uncertain in his own mind whether he is man or boy. His emotions are heightened and, as we have seen, he is vulnerable to criticism and comment, a fear which he sometimes tries to hide behind an aggressive pose; he is idealistic and beginning to question established codes and practices; he wants to earn a place in society and gains satisfaction from helping others. Above all, he has a "need to be needed." The situation can be summed up by saying that our boy/youth has now become conscious of himself as a person.

There are, of course, other pressures to which this age group is subjected in the course of its natural development. The rapidly growing boy becomes conscious and aware of the physical changes that are taking place in his own body and he becomes very much alive to the wonders of sex. He is now becoming interested in girls. He is reserved and reticent about such matters, especially with adults, but enjoys the exhilaration that he derives from the realisation of these growing physical powers within himself. He appreciates that all this is a sign of approaching maturity and enjoys being treated as a man.

THE SCOUT

Our boy/youth is normally quite capable of dealing with the various problems that confront him at this particular stage and is intensely sensitive to anything or anybody who fails to recognise these growing-up manifestations as a perfectly natural stage in his development.

We have noted the tendency of this particular age group to become withdrawn and almost suspicious of adults. He is still, however, responsive to guidance and advice which is given by men whose qualities he admires. These men are often to be found outside his immediate family circle where the intimacy of everyday living sometimes inhibits him. He is equally unresponsive to anything that savours of sentimentality or sloppiness and he dislikes being made a fuss of or patronised. It follows, then, that the Scout will look for and expect a quality of leadership from his Scouters that will stand up to all of these requirements and he will not accept excuses or reasons for its absence. Such arguments as shortage of manpower or the necessity to accept lower standards of leadership in a large and mainly voluntary Movement mean nothing to him — and rightly so. In short, he will expect to find a high standard of leadership in Scouting and, if this is not forthcoming, is likely to seek it elsewhere — and few would blame him for so doing.

When discussing the younger boy in the age range covered by the Scout section we stated that he had little or no spontaneous desire to serve others. As he grows, however, the situation in this respect gradually appears to change and he begins to become aware of responsibilities to the world in which he is growing up. He sees himself slowly fitting into society as an individual, and one of the important tasks of Scouting ought to be to help him to adjust himself to other people and so towards the development of right human relationships. He begins the process which will last for the rest of his life of "needing to be needed" and it is this very "need" that can be channelled into a desire to serve. It may start, initially, with a natural wish to display his knowledge and ability to his younger brothers and blossom, ultimately, into more general forms of service. But, in this, he must have the assurance that what he is doing is worthwhile and worthy of his efforts — he has no time for service for the sake of service. For example — going to a hospital for the set purpose of rendering service and being asked to do the washing up when he gets there may have a temporary attraction but this will soon fade — he sees himself doing something more vital and yet well within his powers and capabilities. How often have we seen this demonstrated in splendidly executed services which have been carried out by teams of Scouts and individual Scouts who have been asked to do jobs which have called forth qualities of endurance, "stickability" and real endeavour. How often, too, have we seen groups of young men inspired with the wish to serve and, because of lack of understanding, discouraged because they have not been asked to carry out what they considered to be man-sized jobs. One of Scouting's most important roles is to train young men; to help develop within them the natural desire to serve and then, where possible, to provide the means and the opportunities for putting the desire into effect. Tackled in the right way it will not find its efforts unrewarded. Chapter 15 deals with the subject of Service Activities very fully and the Service Badges in the Scout Proficiency Badge Schemes have been devised with their main purpose of encouraging the desire to serve in the older Scout.

We would not be facing up to reality if we failed in this particular chapter to mention something about the Scout and his religious faith and belief. This is probably one of the most difficult problems which confronts the boy and young man of Scout age but should, like every other aspect of life for the Scout, be faced. The relevant rule of the Scout Movement states quite categorically that "each invested member of the Movement shall be encouraged to make every effort to progress in his understanding and observance of his Promise 'To do my duty to God,' to belong to some religious body, and to carry into daily practice what he professes." How does this affect the Scout? Well, the rule and its commitment appears clear-cut and allows for little compromise. Nevertheless, we should be careful of the danger of getting religious policy matters out of proportion, realising at the same time that Scouting is not a purely religious Organisation. But duty to God is of fundamental importance and is, therefore, emphasised as an essential requirement of membership.

The average boy as he grows into his teens is invariably faced with difficulties concerning his religious beliefs. Questions and doubts assail him — "Is there a God?" "What proof is there of the existence of God?" "How can I set my life in the right direction?" "How can I keep on the right course?" "How can I make my life what God wants that life to be?" "What is right and wrong?" are but a few of the questions he is likely to ask. When such questions as these are put by the Scout they show that he is beginning to think about some of the deeper and more serious things of life and it is at this stage that his Scouters step in by "encouraging him to make every effort to progress in his understanding and observance of his Promise, 'To do my best to do my duty to God.' " Having said this, though, we would emphasise yet again that the Scout needs sympathetic understanding as he passes through this period of doubt and uncertainty and, with this regard, it is of interest to record that a body which is called the Religious Advisory Board at Scout Headquarters advises that: "Rules should not be so rigid as to require them to leave the Movement; the aim should be to help them."

We would, therefore, summarise all this as far as the Scout is concerned by suggesting that provided the Scout is honestly and sincerely continuing his search for the truth, he can in all honour take the Scout Promise. At the same time it is hoped that eventually, aided by Scouting's teachings and practices, the Scout may arrive at the point where he happily accepts God without doubt or reservation. This will involve him in religious obligations such as attendance at Church Parades. The average boy is not, by nature, religiously minded. He is not normally enthusiastic about Church attendance at any time but this is part of his training as a Scout and every encouragement should be given to him. The Rules state that attendance by Scouts of various forms of religion at a combined Service is allowed with the permission of the District Commissioner and religious authorities concerned — such attendance should, however, be voluntary. Here the matter of Church Parades and Scout Parades generally can be mentioned. Frankly, parades of any kind are not viewed with very great favour by the majority of Scouts today and their views ought to be respected. Nevertheless, it is part of a Scout's training that he should, at times, appear as part of an organised body on ceremonial occasions. When these occur, and in spite of his natural dislike of parades, he will not wish the Movement to which he belongs to suffer in comparison with any other Youth Organisation or Movement. He likes to feel that he belongs to a "good show" and, therefore, when such occasions occur it is essential that they be well planned, organised and rehearsed. It is certain, too, that even today when anything savouring of discipline and regimentation is unpopular, a normal Scout still likes to be smart when the occasion warrants and every encouragement ought to be given to this desire. It is as true today as it ever was that boys still respond to good, sensible discipline and firm leadership provided that it is put over in the right way. They do not like, or admire, poor standards — in anything.

We would end this vital and important part of the chapter with this advice, in the hope that it may help Scouters to point the way for their Scouts. Religion means that, just as the ship's captain relies on the ship's compass to guide and to keep him on the right course, although he cannot actually see the mysterious forces at work on the compass needle, so must our Scouts be brought to rely on the unseen forces of God which can and will guide and govern their lives and keep them on the right course as they sail across the sea of life.

In this chapter we have attempted to provide a picture of the Scout as he is today. This is the typical boy and young man with which the Scout section will be working now and in the years ahead and it would be wrong to ignore the background against which he is living. Changes in the social and economic life of the country and, indeed, the world take place almost daily. The old influences for good such as the family and the church are no longer as strong as they were — excessive materialism abounds. Only a few years ago the Albemarle Report on the Youth Service stated that "there does not seem to be at the heart of society a courageous and exciting struggle for a particular and spiritual life — only a passive, neutral commitment of things as they are." In spite of all this, perhaps because of it, the role that Scouting can play in the lives of boys and young men may become more important than it has ever been.

Fortunately the fundamental characteristics of boyhood are essentially the same as they ever were. His nature, his trust, his humour, his desire for adventure, his impetuousness, instability, inquisitiveness, love of life, appreciation of goodness remain. But he has been brought up in an age of specialisation and has been encouraged to expect high standards in the things that are offered to him — and his training as a Scout is no exception to this. He will not, for long, be satisfied with Scouting if it fails to meet his needs which are, primarily, for fun, for technical skills and knowledge and for adventurous living. The means whereby these requirements are met should be of the highest order too — and the facilities offered to him. He is for ever moving forward and his vision widens; he cannot stand still. Above all, perhaps, he wants to make progress so that eventually he can become a man with all the glamour and the responsibility that he attaches to this adult status.

Before all this takes place our young man, having spent five years as a Scout — five tumultuous and exciting years of mental and physical development — will be looking forward with eager anticipation to the pleasures of Venture Scouting. This should be the aim; whether it becomes reality will depend almost entirely upon his having been satisfied with what has been provided for him during his years as a Scout. Then, as a Venture Scout, he will be able to complete his Scout training. Happy Venture Scouting!

Chapter 4

THE SCOUT LEADER

In St. Luke's Gospel, chapter twenty-two, we read: "But he that is greatest among you, let him be as the younger; and he that is chief, as he that doth serve."

The quotation sets the pattern for this chapter as having in the previous one considered the boy and young man — the Scout — we now turn to the adult who leads him — the Scout Leader.

On the Scout Leader falls the responsibility of organising the Scout Troop into an effective, lively and flexible medium for training the 11 to 16-year-old Scout.

The past history of Scouting produced a "Scoutmaster" who was usually more proficient than his Scouts in most of the skills required for the progressive badge scheme and the average Troop programme then in existence. Consequently he was able to teach and lead nearly every activity undertaken by his Troop. Indeed, many of them believed quite sincerely that it was their personal responsibility and privilege to do so. But circumstances have changed and having regard to the much wider range of activities which are included in the present training scheme it is obvious that it is well-nigh impossible for one man to be proficient in every sphere. Scouts are now given a very wide choice of activities and interests which cater for their individual needs and aspirations and these are no longer limited or restricted by the capabilities and personal interests of the Scout Leader. This means that for some activities the Scout Leader will have to rely on expert instructors and accept that he will not necessarily know more than his Scouts about every activity which they may care to undertake.

Accepting this, it cannot be stressed too much that it is the personal responsibility of the Scout Leader to foster the development of character, personality and capability of each individual member of his Troop. To do this effectively he should lead and co-ordinate the work of a team of adult and Scout instructors rather than expect to achieve his objectives by personal instruction. Naturally, though, he should play some part in this and, indeed, he will want to do so. Again, if he is to give his Scouts the full benefit of the Training Scheme, the Scout Leader should accept that his Troop cannot remain an entirely self-contained unit because his Scouts may at times wish to take part in adventures and expeditions with other Scouts outside their own Troop — under leadership other than his own. He should, in fact, give every encouragement and inducement to his Scouts to join in specialist courses and expeditions, outside their own Troop, as part of their normal Scout training.

From what has been written in this chapter so far it might appear that the chief requirements of the Scout Leader are that he should be merely a co-ordinator and administrator. This, however, would be a completely false appreciation of his task. He will require qualities of character and understanding which are far more important than organisational and administrative efficiency and ability — vital though these may be. Scouts will look to him during the period that they are from 11 to 13 years of age as a pattern on which to mould their own lives and this, inevitably, may mean some form of hero-worship. Later, during the 14 to 16 years period, they will expect from him help and guidance in sorting out many of the problems of growing up and of their adjustment to the adult world. This world today is one in which material things appear to be of more importance than those of the spirit and such things as wealth, position, authority and an easy life are often considered to be the main aims of life. Parents, too, are generally younger than they once were and tend to abnegate responsibility for their young. This often means that when the youngster himself desperately needs, at the age of 14—16, a guiding hand his parents are sometimes unwilling to meet this need. Against a background of moral standards so often based on selfishness and lack of concern for others, the task of leadership of the young is not easy — ask the average teacher or, indeed, anyone who is responsible for the training of adolescents.

The Scout Leader should be a realist who appreciates all the factors and influences which affect the Scouts he leads and should know something about them as they concern each individual in his Troop — and the home background is of vital importance. Because the home plays such a large part in a boy's life it ought to be the aim of the Scout Leader to get to know the parents or guardians of his Scouts as well as possible. In many ways their respective tasks go hand-in-hand — or ought to — for the Scout's happiness is their joint concern. Nevertheless, the Scout Leader should always remember, at least in the majority of cases, that he is very much the junior partner in the team and try to co-operate with the boy's parents as much as he possibly can. The boy is their son and the wise Scout Leader will not try to assume a role in the Scout's life which does not acknowledge this. The situation should be one in which Scout Leader and parents understand each other and co-operate to the full and, in this, a Scout's responsibility to his parents first will be paramount. This will be the normal situation but there may be isolated cases where a Scout's parents are dead or not concerned about their son's welfare. In such situations the Scout Leader's responsibilities may well be much greater but, here again, he will do all that he can to co-operate with the Scout's guardians, teachers or anyone else who may be responsible for his upbringing.

Now a word about the religious policy of the Scout Movement, as it affects the Scout Leader. We have seen in the previous chapter that, "Each invested member of the Movement shall be encouraged to make every effort to progress in his understanding and observance of his Promise, 'To do my best to do my duty to God,' to belong to some religious body, to carry into daily practice what he professes." This implies quite clearly that the Scout Leader ought to be an active member of some religious body and, when he applies for his warrant, the District Commissioner will assure himself that the Scout Leader is fully aware that he will be expected by his personal example to implement this rule. It is important that this requirement is clearly understood for training on the basis of the Scout Law and Promise depends on a good example from adult leaders in this as in all other aspects of living.

All this opens the door to other direct qualities of leadership that are required by the Scout Leader. Many books have been written and many lectures delivered about this vital subject and there are indications that the circumstances which surround modern life, however beneficial they may be in many directions, do not create the conditions which develop qualities of leadership. It is still, however, essential that the youth of our country should receive a lead and an example that will inspire them and help them towards a good life — a life which acknowledges the fact that all humanity is a team and the matter of everyday living a combined effort. Scouting is a Movement which sets out to provide fun and adventure for boys and young men but, with all this, it seeks to encourage the ideas that we are dependent upon one another, that our coming here was no mere accident, that we all have a definite part to play in the overall plan. The guidance that Scouts receive to these ends is of the greatest importance and the example set by the adults who lead them vital. Youth, for all its lack of experience, possesses very clear vision in certain directions, it is discriminating and is able to see through such things as hypocrisy and insincerity very quickly. The wool cannot be pulled over its eyes for very long and the "do as I say not as I do" approach to life is anathematic to it. This means that if Scouts are ever given reason to doubt the integrity, honesty, fairness and sincerity of their Scout Leader, no matter how good he may be in other directions, his effectiveness as a leader will be negligible.

The responsibility this entails is immense for, as we have seen, the Scout Leader is likely to be the subject of hero-worship by the younger boys in his Troops and later regarded as guide, philosopher, counsellor and friend by the older Scouts. Let it here be emphasised that this does not mean that his Troop will expect him to be perfect or a paragon of virtue — neither will they expect him to know all the answers. What they must expect, though, is a man whom they can trust implicitly.

This means that the Scout Leader must be a person to whom his Scouts can look, at all times, with complete confidence. They will expect from him fair decisions unfettered by any bias or favouritism. Naturally he will have a liking for some of his Scouts more than others, but he should never display this openly. Favouritism by him is one of the surest ways of creating unhappy relationships within the Troop and he should never, under any circumstances, succumb to the temptation to become popular for the *sake* of popularity. Granted all this, it is the experience of the writer, that Scouts will submit to discipline and accept correction in the knowledge that their leader is doing what he considers is in *their* best interests — even though they might not always agree at the time. To illustrate this, one need only cite the many examples which Scout Leaders are able to provide from their past experiences. These experiences tell of old Scouts who have come to them in later life and said that they had not been able to understand at the time why their Scouter had done or said this or that but that now, as mature men, they were able to appreciate and value the reasons for the Scouter's actions.

Here are two short incidents taken from life which illustrate the sort of everyday problems which are likely to face a Scout Leader while he is doing his job. A Scout who had to travel a fair distance from home to get to his Troop H.Q. arrived at Troop Meeting looking very pleased with himself. The Scout Leader asked him why he was so happy on this particular evening. "Well," said the Scout, "I came here by bus and I got off without the conductor collecting my fare." Another Scout was lighting a fire in the Patrol Den with some dry pieces of wood which the Scout Leader knew could not have come from the vicinity of the Headquarters. In reply to the Leader's question about the wood the Scout said, "Oh, my Dad whipped it from work and brought it home on the back of his bicycle!"

Sometimes, however, it is not the Scout who presents problems which require tactful handling, but the Leader himself. The Commissioner was visiting a Troop in his District. The Scout Leader was obviously very proud of his Troop and took pleasure in showing off his Scouts to the District Commissioner. It was a good Troop and the District Commissioner was impressed until he was shown a large collection of Troop logs which contained records of all that had taken place over a long period of time. These logs were all written in Stationery Office books — the source from which they came obvious to all who examined them. The District Commissioner knew that the Scout Leader was employed as a civil servant! We wonder how this Scout Leader could have talked to his Scouts with conviction upon Scout Law 1 ('A Scout is to be trusted') and Law 7 ('A Scout has respect for himself and for others') !

Baden-Powell, when writing about the subject of leadership, said, "The leader must have whole-hearted faith and belief in the rightness of his cause," and also, "That he must have a cheery, energetic personality, with sympathy and friendly understanding of his followers." These qualities cannot be overstressed, for such characteristics breed confidence and go a long way towards ensuring the enthusiastic co-operation of those who follow. The Scout Leader should not, however, be a fanatic but rather a man with a balanced outlook on life — preferably with other interests apart from Scouting. His object is to help educate his Scouts in such a way that they, too, will become well balanced, responsible adults and they will appreciate the fact that their Scout Leader identifies himself with them in some of their other activities and interests such as sport, music and hobbies which are not directly connected with Scouting. They will value, too, his interest in their social contacts and relationships with other people — not least of which may well be their early "flutters" with the opposite sex. In the latter, though, he will always seek to encourage the idea that girls and indeed all members of the fairer sex should be treated with courtesy and respect at all times. Friendly banter is one thing — coarseness and any suggestion of vulgarity not being countenanced — and his *own* example in such matters will be of the greatest importance.

What about the Scout who swears or uses bad language? Here, again, the subject ought to be handled with tact and understanding. Maybe the young man comes from a home in which swearing is an everyday occurrence within his house. Care must be exercised, for each Scout requires individual treatment and understanding and the Scout Leader should never reprimand any of his Scouts in front of his colleagues. Nothing is worse for the person concerned and when correction or discipline is necessary — as necessary it will be at times — the Scout should be taken aside and spoken to quietly. The Scout Leader who loses his temper will lose a lot else besides. In these matters, as with others, the background, home environment and all other circumstances that are likely to influence a Scout should be carefully borne in mind before any judgment is made or action taken. Understanding and encouragement to do better should be the principal feature of any correction and, what is more, punishment without *love* in the mind of the punisher will be valueless.

Having said all this, it is important to emphasise that the Scout Leader should always have the courage to assert himself in matters of discipline when the occasion warrants and his Scouts will respect him the more for doing so.

Elsewhere in this book — in chapter 20 — there is evidence of the importance which the Scout Movement quite rightly lays upon the subject of training. The age of "dedicated incompetence" has passed — if it ever existed — and the pattern of life demands higher standards of knowledge and technical ability than ever before. Today, however, there is an *extra* field of study for the adult leader — he needs to know more than ever about the psychological influences and pressures that fall upon those he seeks to lead and an understanding of the mental processes that affect them. He is needed as a philosopher as well as a friend.

Dr. B. R. Wilson, Reader in Sociology at Oxford University, in a recent Charles Russell Memorial Lecture about the Social Context of the Youth Problem said: "Our contemporary young people have been socialised in a child-oriented society in which the child has come to be recognised as a supremely important being upon whom parental affection is lavished. But, although our teenagers are urgently keen to grow up, they want also to cling to the advantages of early childhood. Our society has somehow concentrated familial love into the early years of the child's life, and leaves little over for the still only half-socialised adolescent. Small children, we know, feel themselves to be the very centre of the world from their earliest days. Socialisation and education are processes which should steadily disabuse the child of this illusion, and help it to learn the need for reciprocal respect among men. But in our society we encourage indulgent patterns of child-rearing, perhaps allowing the child to go on believing himself to be the centre of the universe, with inadequate processes of progressive discipline which will allow him to win the balance of loving and being loved which he will need in later life. It is the adolescent who suffers both from the continued illusion and from lack of preparation for exposure to a society which proceeds institutionally rather than affectively. The teenager experiences the shaft of shifting from affective indulgence to affective abandonment. We ought not to be surprised if he continues to claim indulgence and if, when no longer indulged, he indulges himself."

The Scout Leader with the wide age range of the five vital and important years between 11—16 will need to have an appreciation of the truth of Dr. Wilson's observations, for these have a considerable bearing upon his particular sphere of responsibility. Thus it is that we say that, in addition to the usual requirements of leadership in Scouting, knowledge of the skills, practices and techniques, he will need, perhaps more urgently, to have an appreciation of the psychological importance and responsibilities of his task. In these he will co-operate very closely with parent, teacher, minister or clergyman and any other authority responsible for the upbringing of his Scouts and will not, at any time, regard himself as a substitute for them.

There is one further point that ought to be made before we close this chapter. Scouting when it started was intended primarily to be a game for boys and young men — a game with a sense of purpose — but still chiefly a means of bringing happiness and fun into the lives of those who chose to become Scouts. This is as true today as it ever was and means that the Scout Leader should be a man who himself possesses a sense of humour, and a deep appreciation of the fun of Scouting. Without this he will never be a real success for his charges do not become Scouts primarily because they desire to be trained to "take a constructive place in society." They want a leisure-time occupation that will meet their needs and they see in camping and fire-lighting, in the companionship and friendship, in the fun and happiness and in the challenge and adventure of Scouting, a means of satisfying these requirements of boyhood and young manhood. The Scout Leader will run his Troop with tact, understanding, humour and the experience gained from his knowledge of life and example in such a way that he combines all these requirements of youth, and ultimately helps in the production of a young man who is able in every sense to take a constructive place in society.

A challenging and difficult task? Yes, but how abundantly worthwhile !

Chapter 5

THE PATROL SYSTEM

WHAT IT IS

The Patrol System is a means of encouraging boys to plan and carry out activities under the leadership of someone in their own age group. The older members take responsibility, make decisions and train the younger; the younger, in turn, respect, learn from and try to follow the older. It is not merely a method of organising a Troop into convenient, efficient groups for games but a unique method of training for and in leadership. It was considered revolutionary when first introduced but is now widely accepted far beyond the realms of Scouting and remains one of the strongest features of the Scout method. It demonstrates, through the Patrol Leaders' Council, the principles of democracy at work and teaches boys to develop their interests through a challenging programme of training in self-reliance, responsibility and teamwork.

HOW TO ACHIEVE IT

As a method of training, the Patrol System is not an artificial, mechanical device that will run by itself like a water cooling system in a car. Its success will depend on leadership provided by the Scout Leader who seeks to influence by example, encouragement and suggestion and not by the one who attempts to rule the roost. *The Patrol Leader's Handbook* provides a working blueprint for Patrol organisation and activities but the Patrol Leader who organises Patrol Meetings, plans expeditions and produces Scout Standards without any guidance from his Scout Leader will be a rare character indeed.

In a new Troop or one where the Patrol System has not been fully developed in the past, it may take some time to achieve results — perhaps two or three years before the Patrol Leaders become Scouts trained to accept the increasing degree of responsibility which the System demands. The Patrol Leaders' Council should meet regularly to formulate the programme and policy of the Troop. The next step is to use the *Patrol* as the unit for training, games, competitions, camps and service projects. *Communicate* with your Scouts through their Patrol Leader, without removing yourself from the boys completely. Arrange *training sessions* for your Patrol Leaders to provide them with the necessary skills to teach their Patrols. *Adventure activities* for the older Scouts, away from their Patrols and with boys of their own age, will provide an outlet for their more advanced physical and mental development.

PATROL LEADERS

The choice of the right kind of boy for the position of Patrol Leader is vital. Patrol Leaders are Scouts who are learning to lead; they are not necessarily, and probably only rarely, natural leaders. The qualities to look for in choosing a Patrol Leader are many, and seldom will they all be found in one boy. Enthusiasm, ambition, personality, moral integrity, reliability, vitality, commonsense, discretion, imagination, loyalty — but above all the Scout whom you can trust, the one who will work with you to give his Patrol Scouting in the fullest sense of the word. He will need to be knowledgeable in Scouting. He will be training his Patrol in the requirements of the Scout Standard and you may therefore consider the Advanced Scout Standard a minimum requirement. If he's actively working for the Chief Scout's Award himself the members of his Patrol are more likely to take their training seriously too.

It is not always the oldest, nor the most experienced Scout in the Patrol, who will make the best leader; look for the boy who will be accepted by the Patrol, the one by whom they want to be led. The Scout who shows himself as a natural leader in games should also be able to lead when it's raining in camp. In making your selection take care to avoid favouritism; consult the Scouts in the Patrol and talk the matter over fully at the Patrol Leaders' Council and with your Assistants before coming to a decision.

The Patrol Leader must be encouraged to delegate work in the Patrol to his Scouts, giving them increasing degrees of responsibility as they progress through the Patrol. In this way the Patrol System, if it is used correctly, will help to produce leaders.

While all this is going on the Scout Leader should be looking twelve months or so ahead, encouraging the younger Scouts in their training and thus be preparing for the next generation of leaders when they are required.

TRAINING THE PATROL LEADER

It is the Scout Leader's responsibility to train his Patrol Leaders. He should allow them ample scope to put this training into practice in the activities of the Troop. He should use his Assistants and call on the services of Instructors and outside experts for specialist subjects, or projects. Patrol Leaders and Assistant Patrol Leaders should be given the opportunity to attend District Training Courses before, or soon after, their appointment but these should be regarded as supplementary to, and not a substitute for, Patrol Leader training in the Troop. This training must be both enjoyable and instructive and cover a wide range of interests. Practical demonstration and advice on preparation of Patrol activities can be of real benefit and, throughout this training, the Patrol Leader should be made aware of and encouraged to accept the responsibilities of leadership, particularly in regard to providing an attractive and interesting programme for the Patrol.

Training sessions can be held on Troop Night when the rest of the Scouts have gone home, or preferably on a separate evening in the week. These should, first of all, provide the opportunity for Patrol Leaders to keep ahead in the Progress Scheme and should contain sessions covering sections of the Advanced Scout Standard and Chief Scout's Award. If Troop programme themes are discussed at the Patrol Leaders' Council and worked into imaginative activities by the Scout Leader and his Assistants, these training sessions will enable the Patrol

Leaders to prepare for their part in putting the programme into action, both at Troop Meetings and when they are working with their Patrols.

By forming the Patrol Leaders into a 'Patrol' with the Scout Leader as 'Patrol Leader' it is possible to give instruction in the necessary technical skills and to demonstrate activities which can be run with the Patrol. If discussion and questions follow, the Scout Leader can suggest further ideas for developing the subject and will see if his Patrol Leaders have learned sufficient from the training to run this effectively with their Scouts. The Scout Leader can advise on the use of visual aids and explain demonstration techniques. The Patrol Leader, by watching the methods used by the Scout Leader will learn how to give clear, concise instructions and the art of delegating in order to use his Patrol to the best effect.

It may not be possible to cover all the subjects in the training programme in this way. Patrol Leaders can be encouraged to specialise in subjects of their choice and teach these skills to the other Patrols. With the more advanced subjects such as canoeing and sailing, Assistant Scout Leaders, Instructors and outside experts can be used to train the Patrol direct; the Patrols will benefit from this expert instruction and the Patrol Leaders, too, will derive much from seeing another Instructor with their Patrol. To keep the Patrol Leaders ahead try and give them some preliminary training in a subject you propose dealing with in this way.

Apart from these regular sessions, week-end camps can give additional training and help you to get to know and understand the problems of your Patrol Leaders. A week-end camp, held in the Spring, in preparation for camping and outdoor activities of the Summer months could include projects to test the training and initiative of your Patrol Leaders and activities which they can try out before putting into action in their own programmes. If you invite the Assistant Patrol Leaders to share this week-end you will have sufficient numbers to form at least two Patrols and emphasise the importance of their position in 'assisting' to lead the Patrols in the Troop. To leave more time for training it helps if you have a small staff of Assistant Scout Leaders, Instructors or members of your Service Unit to cook certain meals during the week-end — and their additional help in staffing projects and activities will be available.

Other week-end activities can provide the Patrol Leader with experience in the wider aspects of Troop programme planning. If the Patrol Leaders and Scouters together go to find camp sites for Troop camps this demonstrates to them and to their Scouts the executive position they hold in the Troop. If such a week-end is not all 'action' but a series of fruitless calls at first, the Patrol Leader will learn the frustrations and difficulties which are often the prelude to a successful venture. Special activities for the older members of the Troop will give the Patrol Leader time to relax with others of his own age away from the responsibilities of his Patrol, and provide activities appropriate to his own level of training and physical capabilities. These activities do not necessarily have to be organised from within the Troop and at this stage in his development specialist courses arranged by outside experts may well meet the needs of the older boy.

The status of the Patrol Leader will grow in the eyes of his Scouts if the Scout Leader is seen to give him responsibility and small privileges like remaining after Troop Meeting and staying up in camp a little later than the rest for a "cuppa" with the Scouters will work wonders. Criticism of the Patrol Leader in front of his Patrol will lower him in their estimation more than anything else. A quiet word with him afterwards will sort most problems out — if you have chosen the right Scout for the job.

It will be found that *The Patrol Leader's Handbook* provides plenty of ideas but few Patrol Leaders will be able to translate them into action on their own. The Scout Leader must be ready to give the initial impetus and to follow this up with a regular flow of encouragement and guidance.

EFFECT ON THE SCOUTS

In the smaller unit of the Patrol, a Scout can receive individual attention which it is impossible to give him in a larger unit. He will learn to work as a member of a team, doing things with others for a common purpose. The age range within this Patrol will bring him in contact with a wider circle of friends and he will be led by a Scout in the same broad age group in which he finds himself at school. The Patrol is an extension of a boy's natural desire to be an accepted member of a gang. He will be offered increasing degrees of responsibility within the Patrol until he is ready to assume leadership himself. Every Scout should be encouraged to take responsibility for a job in the Patrol; older boys can help the younger ones at first but, even so, every Scout should feel he has responsibility for *something*, however small, and, because of this, is needed by the others. As a Scout progresses through the Patrol he should have the opportunity to try all the jobs — Treasurer, Quartermaster food and gear, Secretary, Librarian, First-aider; in this way he will know something about and understand the problems of each appointment should he become Patrol Leader in the future. The Patrol Leader chooses his own Assistant and will want to discuss this with the Scouts in his Patrol, the Patrol Leaders' Council and his Scout Leader. An Assistant Patrol Leader should be a Scout who will work in harmony with the Patrol Leader who, in turn, should be ready to share with him his plans, ambitions and ideas for the Patrol. If the Assistant is allowed to lead certain activities on his own, this will give him valuable experience if in the future he takes full responsibility for the Patrol. The Patrol Leader may have to miss some meetings due to homework and other commitments; his Assistant can only be of real help if he is in the Patrol Leader's confidence and ready to take over should the need arise.

The question of placing Scouts in Patrols is one that should receive the careful consideration at regular intervals of all Leaders in the Troop. The Link Badge will help the Scout Leader and Patrol Leader to get to know the Cub Scout entrant some time before he comes up into the Troop. He may have pals in a particular Patrol, boys from his school or who live near his home, and may express a preference for being with them. Boys from outside the Movement are sometimes encouraged to join by friends who are already in the Troop and, quite naturally, they will want to be in the same Patrol. Be ready to recognise existing friendships in this way although it may mean uneven numbers in some Patrols for a time. It is often wise to tell a new Scout that his first Patrol is a 'temporary' one until he has had time to settle down and look around. Young Scouts tend to change their friendships quite often and the Scout Leader should be ready to suggest a move to another Patrol where this is clearly to the advantage of all concerned, at the same time endeavouring to avoid the regular request from the boy who wishes to change Patrols every time his Patrol Leader tells him to do the washing up! The Patrol System can help to develop new friendships, too, and here is something which should be encouraged when the occasions arise.

EFFECT ON PATROL LEADER

The Patrol Leader is presented with a challenge in leadership and the chance to prove to himself and to others that he can measure up to it. The progressive scheme of training has given him the basic skills; by extending and widening his programme of training and through working with his Patrol he will be prepared for and learn some of the problems to be faced in leading others. He will learn to organise a group of boys of different abilities and temperaments in the carrying out of projects that will test them individually and as a team. He will experience the work of a committee and learn to make decisions for the benefit of others and not always for himself. In the training and activity sessions he arranges for his Patrol he will practise the ideals of service to others and lead his Patrol in service projects both within and outside the Movement. He will not be left to achieve all this on his own, for guidance will be available to him through the Patrol Leaders' Council and his Scout Leader. In all this the Patrol Leader must not neglect his other duties; the time he gives to his Patrol and to Scouting must never interfere with his home life, academic studies and other interests, and the Scout Leader will need to keep a careful watch to see that this does not happen.

EFFECT ON THE TROOP

The Scout Troop is a collection of Patrols and is only as good as its Patrol activities. Where the Patrol System is running successfully the Patrols will be proud of their identity and, as a result, games, competitions and activities will be more lively.

Scouts will see that teamwork in the Patrol produces results and will be more determined to work together in their efforts to win. The progress scheme of training can be stimulated by including specific subjects or skills in competitions. These should be run over short periods, as Scouts will tend to lose interest if competitions are allowed to drag on. These activities should never be regarded as an end in themselves, but should be run for the Scouts — for their enjoyment and to stimulate their training. The Patrol System may not always produce a highly efficient Troop where everything runs smoothly like a well-oiled engine, but it is the Scout method and the results in individual character training will outweigh the advantages that can be seen on the surface from a Troop working solely under the direction and orders of the Scout Leader.

EFFECT ON PARENTS

It is essential that when a boy first joins a Troop his parents are helped to understand the reasons for arranging the Scout training programme through the Patrol System. A personal interview between the Scout Leader and the parents is the best method to achieve understanding and time spent in this way will rarely be wasted. Meetings for parents of new Scouts to discuss uniforms, activities, subscriptions, etc., can also give the Scout Leader and the Patrol Leaders an opportunity to meet parents. Introductory pamphlets published by Headquarters and Group typewritten handouts can be used to provide parents with information concerning the aims of the Movement and the activities of the Troop which their sons are joining.

Camp Meetings and Open Nights can show the Patrol System in action, if they are arranged to include well-rehearsed Patrol activities where leadership and teamwork are necessary for success. Film shows of Troop and Patrol activities with the Patrol Leaders giving commentaries, will demonstrate the value and also the achievements of the Patrol System. A Group Magazine, or regular News-sheet, with comment on Troop and Patrol activities and details of future projects, will ensure that accurate information is reaching parents and encourage them to take an interest in these matters.

The Patrol System is an integral part of the Scout Movement and Scouting without the Patrol is not real Scouting. If we are to succeed in our objective the Scout Leader's thinking and the training programme must, therefore, centre round the basic unit which is the Patrol.

Chapter 6

PATROL ACTIVITIES

The Patrol System will only be fully effective if the Patrols organise and carry out their own activities, in addition to those in which they take part on a Troop basis. Scouts learn the importance of teamwork through Patrol activities and the Patrol Leader develops his powers of leadership, giving his Scouts increasing degrees of responsibility.

As stated in the previous chapter, few Patrol Leaders will be competent at first to run their Patrols without any assistance from the Scout Leader. Timidity on the part of the Patrol Leader to 'go it alone' with Patrol activities can only be dispelled by affording him the opportunities to prove to himself that he can do this. Patrol projects at Troop Meetings are the best way to start and programmes should be devised to include as many activities on a Patrol basis as possible. The Patrol Leaders will require training at separate sessions to prepare them for putting these projects into action. At Troop Meetings the Scout Leader will be there in the background, on hand if needed and ready to give a word of advice or encouragement afterwards — making a conscious effort *not* to interfere whilst the project is in progress if this can be avoided.

When the Patrol Leaders have gained experience by running projects in this way, they will be ready to undertake activities away from Troop Meetings. Patrol activities only stand a chance of success where Patrol Leaders have available to them a progressive programme of training provided by the Scout Leader and his team. At first it may be necessary not only to provide material for use in activities but also to convince the Patrol Leaders that the ideas are practical and within their capabilities. This can best be achieved by running the activities with the Patrol Leaders forming the Patrol, led by the Scout Leader or his Assistant. These are then used by the Patrol Leaders with their own Patrols. In this way, and if they are encouraged to do so, they will gain confidence and plan their own activities.

PATROL ORGANISATION

The Patrol will need to be a close-knit, working unit in which every Scout has a part to play. Each should be given a job — a worthwhile one and not just a label that carries with it no responsibility. The Quartermaster (gear) looks after the equipment, the Quartermaster (food) plans menus and buys the food, the Librarian keeps the books, magazines, maps, etc., first-aid supplies are looked after by another Scout, the Patrol Treasurer is responsible for subscriptions and accounts and the Secretary keeps the log. With a set-up like this, most of the Scouts in the Patrol will be in a position to make some contribution towards the planning of an activity and to take a more active interest than would be the case if the Patrol Leader did everything himself. The Patrol Leader will need guidance from the Scout Leader in organising his Patrol in this way. In a young Patrol it may be difficult to find sufficient Scouts with experience to tackle these jobs. The Patrol Leader should be encouraged to make these appointments and, if necessary, training can be given to the Scouts concerned by the Scout Leader and his Assistants. If one of the Assistant Scout Leaders is responsible for Troop accounts, he could, in addition, train the Patrol Treasurers, showing them how to keep accounts and check their records every month or so. Another Assistant could train the Patrol Quartermasters — or perhaps the Group Quartermaster would be interested in helping with this. Direct training of Scouts in the Patrol can be beneficial to all concerned and the Patrol Leader will no doubt welcome outside expertise used in this way.

PROGRAMME MATERIAL

There is a wide range of literature available to help with

material for programmes — books published by Scout Headquarters, training articles in *The Scouter* and other magazines and periodicals. The Scout Leader will need to advise on this, perhaps suggesting that subscriptions are taken out and paid for from Patrol funds. Training courses and meetings between Patrol Leaders from other Troops will also help to stimulate interest in a wider range of activities.

EQUIPMENT

Patrols will need certain basic equipment of their own to carry out an active programme. This should be stored in a place where it is readily available at any time during the week. As a minimum, Patrol equipment should include sufficient items to enable the Patrol Leader to train and test his Patrol in the Scout Standard. (This is his particular responsibility in the general Progress Scheme.) In addition, the Patrol will need access to equipment owned by the Troop and Group — camping equipment, pioneering gear, etc. Training Handbooks and proficiency badge books are also important and up-to-date copies should be readily available to all Scouts within the Patrol.

MEETING PLACE

The ideal, of course, is for the Patrol to have a place of its own. This does not have to be large and it is not necessary to find somewhere for the exclusive use of the Patrol. A shed or garage, attic or cellar — all these are possibilities. Provision can sometimes be made for Patrols to meet at the Troop Headquarters or dens can be constructed if the building is owned by the Group. Each Patrol does not need its own room — removable wall decorations can create sufficient atmosphere to allow different Patrols to meet each night of the week and to feel it is 'theirs.' If these ideas are not practical propositions at the moment, Patrols may be able to have indoor meetings in their homes. With a Patrol of eight Scouts running fortnightly Patrol Meetings, this would mean each Scout having a meeting in his home every sixteen weeks. It may not be possible for every Scout to have meetings at home but it is worth trying. Outdoor meetings in the better weather can be arranged in parks, open spaces or local camp sites and throughout the year Patrols should be encouraged to have at least part of their meeting outdoors.

INSTRUCTION

The Scout Leader can help the Patrol Leader to provide a varied activity programme by contacting experts in particular subjects both within and outside the Movement. Group Instructors could be asked to run training courses for Patrols or to give assistance with projects such as canoe building, carpentry, photography, printing and so on. Local Organisations may be prepared to provide speakers or to invite Patrols to their meetings. To make a visit worthwhile it is sometimes best to arrange a joint Patrol Meeting, or to ask the visitor to come to a full meeting of the Troop.

Many subjects in the Progress Scheme will require expert tuition and the Scout Leader will be wise to make contact with experts in this way.

The Patrol Leader's Handbook provides a number of suggestions for the range of Patrol activities and the notes that follow are complementary to the appropriate chapters in that Handbook.

PATROL MEETINGS

Patrol Leaders should be encouraged to run their own meetings regularly. How often these are held will depend on many factors. If the Troop meets every week, a Patrol Meeting once a fortnight is ideal. On the other hand, a Troop Meeting once a month would allow more time for Patrol Meetings and three or four of these each month might be possible. The timing of Patrol Meetings is something to be decided by the Scouts concerned. These timings will, for instance, have to fit in with their other interests, homework, etc. The Scout Leader should satisfy himself that meetings finish on time and that Scouts are not out too late during the week. Use of the Patrol Activity Report Forms illustrated in Chapter 4 of *The Patrol Leader's Handbook* will mean that the Scout Leader knows what his Patrols are doing at their meetings. He will be able to keep a check on attendances in this way too — and this may be vital if Troop Meetings are held at monthly intervals.

Scouts will go to Patrol Meetings if they enjoy themselves

and find purposeful activity. The Scout Leader will, therefore, want to see that his Patrol Leaders are equipped to provide this. The first essential is a good programme which has been well thought out beforehand and written down on paper. The Patrols Leaders' Council might discuss themes of training for Patrol Meetings and the Scout Leader can provide ideas for activities at Patrol Leaders' training sessions. At first, Patrol Leaders will need help in planning their programmes and if the Scout Leader helps with this from the beginning, the Patrol Leader will learn the right way to do things. The Patrol will stand a better chance of having an enjoyable activity and, with experience, will gradually be able to plan and organise on its own, with less reliance on the Scout Leader for ideas.

THE PATROL IN TOWN

Within the environs of the town there is a variety of activities waiting for the Patrol. *Visits* can be arranged to places of interest — from airports and art galleries to waterworks and zoological gardens. *People* can be asked to talk about or demonstrate their hobbies and skills, or may be prepared to give expert instruction in specialist subjects. The town is an excellent background for wide games, trails, and scavenger hunts.

Imaginative observation activities can be used to lead Scouts to otherwise unexplored areas of the town. Interviews, public opinion polls and surveys of all kinds develop a Scout's ability to express himself and converse with adults. The Scout Leader may need to make the contacts initially and this is often advisable to avoid troubling busy people with a number of enquiries from individual Patrol Leaders. The Patrol Leaders should be encouraged to develop the basic ideas, perhaps discussing these with the Scout Leader who may be able to make suggestions for improvement.

THE PATROL IN THE COUNTRY

Full day activities farther afield are good practice for Patrol camps and, in addition, open the door to a wider range of pursuits. Members of the Patrol can take part in the planning — the Quartermaster (gear) assembles the cooking and games equipment, the Treasurer works out the cost and so on. In this way, Patrol jobs become more than labels — each member of the Patrol is dependent on the other and teamwork will begin to be important. Matters of safety should be discussed with the Patrol Leader and the Scout Leader should satisfy himself that parents have been informed of meeting time, equipment needed, cost and approximate time of return. A telephone contact at home is a good plan so that a message can be left if the Patrol is, for any reason, delayed.

Hiking is not an end in itself — for most Scouts at least! A hike should preferably have a purpose — with a number of activities to occupy the varied interests of the Patrol. Headquarters, County and District camp sites can be visited and the facilities they offer used by the Patrol for pioneering, obstacle courses, water activities and so on. The Scout Leader may be able to arrange facilities in woods or on farms for Scouting activities — cooking, backwoods shelters and the like.

Cycling or the use of public transport make a change from hiking and some Patrols may be able to try pony trekking or water transport. Evening activities in the dark are best at week-ends, when there is no school the next day. Particular care is needed with hikes along country roads where poor lighting may endanger a Patrol exposed to road traffic. It's best if the Patrol can keep to known footpaths and avoid roads wherever possible. If they have to walk along roads a light should be carried at the front and rear of the Patrol. With overnight Patrol expeditions, the Scout Leader will need to be satisfied that the Patrol Leader is capable of leading the project, that the Scouts taking part have sufficient experience and that the planning has been adequately carried out.

PATROL PROJECTS

Projects in which a number of Scouts take part can be a useful method of developing interests and hobbies, as well as a means of getting Scouts to work together for a common purpose. The problem of maintaining interest over a long period should be considered and, at first, it is best to encourage the kind of project that can be brought to a conclusion and which shows results within weeks rather than months. The Scout Leader will need to be careful not to force his Patrols to undertake projects in which they have no interest but, wherever possible, should try to draw on their ideas. Competitive projects are a good way to get started — for example: photography, Scout-cars, swimming.

With projects involving technical skills, such as canoe building or radio construction, the Patrol Leader may require expert advice. This could be provided by Venture Scouts or Instructors attaching themselves to the Patrol for a period, or by the use of facilities offered by outside Organisations. Service projects should form part of the regular programme of the Patrol and the Scout Leader's assistance in finding suitable undertakings will be needed. Again, short-term projects are best where the results are readily apparent.

THE PATROL IN CAMP

Patrol activities throughout the year provide the opportunity for training to be given in campcraft. In the summer months, afternoon and evening Patrol Meetings outdoors can cover tent pitching, cooking, oven building, gadget construction and so on. In the winter months, there are still plenty of things to do — menu planning, packing a rucsac, experimenting with weights of equipment, making camp site models and indoor cooking.

The Scout Leader's responsibility for a good standard of Patrol camping is a vital one and he will need to satisfy himself that the type of training carried out and the preparations made are adequate. A young Scout's first camp should be one where there are Scouters present. It is inadvisable to allow a boy who is new to the Troop to go to a Patrol camp until the Scout Leader has satisfied himself that the boy is prepared for this. In many Troops a camp is arranged early in the season, between Easter and Whitsun, for Scouts who have joined during the winter months. The young Scouts in each Patrol camp with their Patrol Leader and his Assistant, each Patrol forming a separate unit. The Scout Leader and his Assistants provide the services and arrange one or two activities, while the Patrol Leaders teach the younger Scouts the basic elements of camping.

Additional camps will be required for Patrol Leaders and their Assistants. These can be held during the winter months, perhaps with indoor accommodation. The emphasis should be on showing the Patrol Leader how to lead his Patrol in camp for he should be sufficiently experienced and knowledgeable in the art of camping by this stage of his progress through the Troop.

The first camp a Patrol Leader arranges on his own should preferably be held on a site where adult help is readily available. A Headquarters, County or District site is probably best, or the Scout Leader may know of a farm where the owner is prepared to keep an eye on things. The Scout Leader or his Assistants will usually want to visit the camp during the week-end. Distance from home and the timing of the camp should, therefore, be considered in relation to the Scouters' other commitments.

Guidance is given in *The Patrol Leader's Handbook* on the preparatory work for camp and, wherever possible, this should be shared by the Scouts in the Patrol. The Scout Leader will want to be satisfied that the planning has been thorough, checking the menu, food, equipment and first-aid lists. A constructive Scouting programme should be planned with a time-table of activities. Meals should be regular and on time, but otherwise the programme should be adaptable. The important point to stress to the Patrol Leader is that a camp without purposeful activity may tend to become boring. If he keeps his Scouts busy with projects that they enjoy there will be little opportunity for them to get into trouble. In all this the Scout Leader will need to be ready to advise and give practical help — the amount of help required varying according to the experience and ability of the individual Patrol Leader.

Careful budgeting should be encouraged and it is best if the Scout Leader checks this before the cost is announced to the Patrol. Parents will need to be fully informed of the camp details, times of departure and return, transport arrangements, equipment, cost, and the address of site. The parents of younger Scouts should be told that an adult is on hand and that the camp will be visited by a Scouter. A high standard of camping and cleanliness is to be expected at Patrol camps.

At a short week-end camp there may not be time for elaborate gadgets, but a simple dresser, table, wash-bowl stand and fireplace should be minimum requirements. The gadgets that are built should have and serve a purpose for the period of the camp. If a good standard of 'simple' gadgetry is encouraged at Patrol camps, it will be a natural progression to more elaborate constructions when there is more time at Troop camps.

How the chores of camp are tackled will be a sign of a Patrol's ability to work as a team and planning a simple rota will help the Patrol Leader to share these round.

TRAINING THE PATROL

The Patrol Leader should be encouraged to take an active part in the training of his Scouts from the time they first make contact with the Troop. If the Scout Leader includes the Patrol Leader in Link Badge and Scout Badge training, this is a good start. Patrol Meeting programmes can include sessions of instruction in the basic skills covered in the Progress Scheme. Where possible, these skills should be taught through activities rather than 'lectures.' Where instruction is necessary in more formal sessions, the Scout Leader should demonstrate to the Patrol Leaders methods of instruction, using visual aids and other means of making the training lively and interesting. Most Patrol Leaders will need guidance in putting this across and use can be made of Patrol Leaders' training sessions to do this.

Certain subjects are preferably taught by specialists and the Scout Leader will be well advised to form a team of Assistant Scout Leaders, Instructors and outside experts to cover these. Members of this team can prepare the Patrol Leaders so that they are equipped to instruct their Patrols or themselves give direct instruction at Patrol Meetings. In addition, courses can be run for Scouts from different Patrols who are ready to receive training and to be tested in their knowledge of a particular section of the Progess Scheme.

The Patrol Leader is responsible for training and testing his Scouts in the requirements of the Scout Standard. He will need to be well versed in the subjects to be covered and will also require training in how to instruct and the standard of achievement to expect. The advice given in *The Patrol Leader's Handbook* will need to be supplemented by the Scout Leader who will know the abilities of the individual Scouts in the Patrol. The emphasis is on training through Patrol activities, with the Patrol Leader playing a major part in this, aided by specialist Instructors. Nevertheless, the Scout Leader will need to take an active interest in the progress of every Scout. Regular review of the training progress of individual Scouts should, therefore, be carried out at the Patrol Leaders' Council.

Chapter 7

THE PATROL LEADERS' COUNCIL

The Patrol Leaders' Council is the debating chamber of the Troop, a forum where opinions and ideas are discussed, problems resolved and decisions made. The Council provides a unique opportunity to demonstrate the procedure of the committee without the necessity for too much formality, where the spirit to give and take produces results.

MEMBERSHIP

All Patrol Leaders are members of the Council and in small Troops Assistant Patrol Leaders may be invited to form a working unit of reasonable size. The Scout Leader, and sometimes the Assistant Scout Leaders, attend meetings in an advisory and counselling capacity, unlike the Patrol Leaders who are primarily delegates representing the views of their Scouts.

PATROL LEADERS' STATUS

The Patrol Leader has an executive position in the running of the Troop, on an equal footing with the Scouters. He will enjoy being a member of the team, holding discussion and being a party to decisions made for the benefit of the Troop. It is vital that he is seen in this role of policy-maker and pacesetter and not as a junior leader acting under the direction of the Scouters who make all the decisions.

The Patrol Leader brings to the Council not only his own views and opinions but, more important, those of his Patrol and Scouts individually. A Patrol in Council Meeting will enable him to obtain the majority view and if this does not coincide with his own opinion he should, nevertheless, put forward the Patrol's decision. In the same way, both he and his Patrol should be ready to accept the majority decision of the Patrol Leaders' Council.

Throughout these deliberations, the Patrol Leader will share the responsibilities of Troop management, find satisfaction in success and gain experience from the things that don't quite work out as planned — but above all he will learn to overcome problems in company with others.

The Senior Patrol Leader will normally be Chairman of the Patrol Leaders' Council or it may be decided to let each Patrol Leader chair the meetings in turn. A good Chairman will need to have the respect of his pals, to be impartial as he guides discussion, businesslike in getting through an agenda, possess a sense of humour and know when to be serious. The Scout Leader will want to spend time guiding and training the Chairman towards fitting himself for the job. It is, therefore, an advantage to have the same Chairman throughout a series of meetings, as confidence will grow with experience.

THE SCOUT LEADER

It is essential for the Scout Leader to work through the Chairman rather than to take the chair himself. The short-cut via dictatorship, benevolent or otherwise, can be tempting, but the Patrol Leaders' Council is not a platform for the Scout Leader's ego. If he places himself in a position where he is more than an adviser or counsellor he will deny to the Patrol Leaders the opportunity and experience of running things for themselves. He can provide items for the agenda and advise on the approach to a particular theme in an endeavour to stimulate discussion — taking part himself without dominating the proceedings. He can suggest alternatives to a course of action which he knows from experience will not have the intended result or decide to keep silent and let them learn by their mistakes. A decision to buy an item of cheap equipment will teach the lesson that quality pays if the Scouter lets them purchase it and then refrains from saying 'I told you so' when it breaks. The Scout Leader retains the right to veto but should aim at never having to use it.

RESPONSIBILITIES

The Patrol Leaders' Council sets standards for the rest of the Troop to follow. This is a corporate responsibility, shared by the Scouters and Patrol Leaders, whose personal example needs to be above reproach if they are to do this effectively.

The approval of the Patrol Leaders' Council is required before a Scout Standard award is made, and the Scout Leader will do well to seek the opinion of the Council before awarding the Advanced Scout Standard or recommending a Chief Scout's Award. This will emphasise that technical ability is not enough but that an understanding of the Law and Promise and the part the Scout plays in his Patrol and Troop life count as well.

The Council will occasionally discuss matters of discipline, remembering that the members of their Patrols are youngsters who are finding their feet in the world and learning to be Scouts. Where there are problems with a particular Scout the reasons for his behaviour should be found and, if no breach of confidence is involved, explained to the Patrol Leaders. It may help to ask an older boy to meet the Patrol Leaders' Council to state his case and to hear for himself their views on his behaviour. Remedies are few for we are a voluntary Movement. A change of Patrol or loss of seniority may be effective; missing an expedition or camp may have a more salutory effect. In these things the Scout Leader will need to temper with justice, and sometimes mercy, the feelings of the Patrol Leaders and be ready to call to see the Scout and his parents afterwards to explain the reasons for a particular course of action.

Competition details and awards are decided at the Patrol Leaders' Council and we should not overlook the good effect to be gained from occasionally asking a Scout to a meeting to be thanked personally or congratulated on a specific achievement which has required some effort on his part.

New members of the Troop from the Cub Scout Pack and

outside the Movement will be mentioned, Link Badge training arranged and decisions taken as to which Patrol they should go in. The appointment of Patrol Leaders and Assistant Patrol Leaders will be discussed.

Troop funds are administered by the Patrol Leaders' Council and a regular report made by the Troop Treasurer who would normally be one of the Assistant Scout Leaders or an Administrator. Decisions are made on future expenditure. An outline training programme for Troop and Patrol activities will be discussed and plans made for expeditions and camps. Service projects should be discussed at Patrol Leaders' Council to avoid duplication of approaches to outside Organisations and to ensure that projects undertaken by Patrols are within their capabilities. Details of Group, District and County events are given by the Scout Leader and the Council discuss the part the Troop will play in these. In all this, not only will decisions be made by the Patrol Leaders' Council but information will be channelled through the Patrol Leader who will be first to give news of future activities to his Patrol. If details are displayed on the notice board or given in the Group Magazine or News-sheet this will act as a reminder and the boring repetition of notices at the end of Troop Meetings become unnecessary.

THE MEETING

Where the meeting is held is for you, the Scout Leader, to decide. Some Troops have a special Council Room in their Headquarters, some hold the meeting at the Scout Leader's home, others visit each Patrol Leader's home in turn. Uniform should be worn. Once a month is about right for full meetings, relying on informal gatherings at other times for week-to-week matters. In camp the Council could meet informally every day.

From the foregoing the need for some formal procedure should be obvious. There should be a Chairman and an Agenda; a Secretary can be appointed from among the Patrol Leaders or they can take turns at this job. Before the meeting the Secretary prepares the Agenda, asking the other Patrol Leaders if they have any special items for inclusion. The Scout Leader and Chairman meet to go through the Agenda together so that the Chairman is fully briefed and does not have to refer to the Scout Leader during the meeting for details of activities. If the Agenda is circulated well before the meeting this gives time for items to be discussed at the Patrol in Council meetings. It helps, too, if the Minutes of the previous meeting can be typed and passed to the members before the next meeting so that they are reminded of the points discussed last time. This may not always be possible to arrange but will certainly give the meeting an added significance and importance to the Patrol Leaders. Efficiency is not to be shunned if it helps to provide purposeful Scouting but, at the other extreme, we should avoid such a welter of paper, propositions and amendments that the whole meeting becomes snowed under.

In *The Patrol Leader's Handbook* specimen Agendas and Minutes are given, with ideas for meetings of the Patrol Leaders' Council. The meeting naturally begins with Prayer — for understanding and guidance in the discussions that will follow. The Minutes of the last meeting are agreed or alterations made to put the record straight. Matters arising from the Minutes are followed by a review of recent activities and projects are planned for the future. Patrol Leaders should be encouraged to give regular reports on their Patrols and be able to state what progress each Scout has made, or account for the lack of it. Finances, Patrol problems, requests for help and so on, the meeting ending with 'other business' where points not appearing on the Agenda can be discussed.

Throughout, the atmosphere should be friendly, with Scouters and Patrol Leaders having equal opportunity to join in discussion and of reaching decisions together. At one time you may be blessed with a fine bunch of Patrol Leaders, good in debate and bubbling over with ideas — and a few months later wonder if it is all worth while when you find yourself with a new Council who appear to be the complete reverse. Patience, understanding and good humour will have their reward if the Scout Leader is prepared to get the Troop to run itself in this way.

In addition to the formal meetings of the Council there will be opportunities for gatherings at other times and these have a complementary part to play. Informal gatherings will emphasise the shared responsibility of Scouters and Patrol Leaders in running the Troop. This, of course, is shown to best advantage in the workings of the Patrol Leaders' Council. However, a few minutes after Troop Meetings or church, an hour during the week or an evening with the latest 'pop' records — in the relaxed atmosphere of these occasions discussion is often less inhibited.

The Patrol Leaders are usually about the same age and have probably known each other throughout their Scouting life. In towns, Scouting might have brought them together and in smaller communities it may well be part of the whole life they share — school, hobbies, church and so on. Each Patrol Leader is an individual with a character of his own; different activities have their own appeal and yet they will get a lot from sharing.

Patrol Leaders need support, encouragement and help, for responsibility weighs heavier on some shoulders than others. A problem shared is a problem halved, yet sometimes Patrol Leaders may be reluctant to do so for fear that this might be interpreted as an admission of weakness in their leadership. By encouraging the Patrol Leaders to get-together informally in this way, the Scout Leader will build up a team of pals who are keen to lead the Troop. A well established Patrol Leaders' Council can surmount problems and difficulties in a way that would be almost impossible to a Scouter working on his own. The Scout Leader who has confidence in the Patrol System will have the satisfaction of seeing it work in practice and of providing himself with an ever-present source of help and encouragement.

Chapter 8

THE SCOUT PROGRESS SCHEME

Since the Movement's earliest days, students of Scouting principles have recognised the Patrol System, with its concept of encouraging boys to plan and carry out worthwhile activities on their own, as one of the soundest characteristics of training in the Scout Troop. It is now widely accepted in other fields, but the Patrol System remains one of the essential features of the Scout method.

Successive teams of planners have sought the means of strengthening the Patrol System by providing schemes of training embracing subjects devised to encourage both individual and collective progress by Scouts and Patrols. In many Troops, however, previous training schemes have tended to produce depressingly poor results. Scout Leaders have found themselves so burdened with carrying out elementary instruction and test-passing that the vital task of training their Patrol Leaders has often been neglected. This in turn has led to Patrol Leaders being inexperienced and incapable of training their Patrols effectively or of leading them in challenging Scouting activities. The situation has been further aggravated by the limitations of the Scout age range, making necessary the appointment of young Patrol Leaders who have generally been too close in age and development to the boys they have tried to lead.

The Scout Progress Scheme takes full advantage of the now wider age range of the Scout Section and the fact that generally the appointment of older Patrol Leaders is practicable, by giving direct encouragement to the wider use of the Patrol System and by placing greater responsibility on the Patrol Leader for training and promoting the progress of the Scouts in his Patrol. The system of training has been specifically drafted to enable all boys to make rapid progress in the early stages, to ensure that most aspire to a reasonable standard of Scouting, and to encourage a high proportion to maintain their progress to a high level of attainment.

SCOUT PROGRESS BOOK

In the past, the only individual record of progress available to Scouts was a card listing only by name the tests for which the Scout could enter. For information on the actual badge requirements it was necessary for the Scout to refer to other publications, but even these separate sources tended only to list the tests and offered little or no indication of the intended purpose of the particular activities.

Today's Scout is better equipped than his predecessors to understand the training scheme and to plan his progress through it. In addition to providing the Scout with a permanent, handy record of his achievements, *The Scout Progress Book* groups the full requirements under concise headings, and lays before him a complete picture of the many activities and pursuits that are open to him as a Scout. The book is so styled that it can be used as a ready-made source of inspiration for the provision of interesting and worthwhile activity at individual, Patrol and Troop level.

Here, of course, the book gives the Scout an indication of the kinds of activities that should properly be included in the Troop programme, and can be used as a weapon to back his legitimate demand for those activities if they are not provided!

For interested people outside the Movement — friends, parents, schoolmasters, potential employers — *The Scout Progress Book* can provide a concise, informative guide to the comprehensive nature of Scout training.

PROGRESSIVE TRAINING

Both by encouraging the new recruit and by catering for the more sophisticated requirements of the older boy, the Scout Progress Scheme is readily suited to the Patrol System. The main features of the scheme are that it enables a boy to play a full part in Scouting activities right from the start; it provides material for active outdoor programmes, including adventure activities for older boys; it offers alternative tests to suit the boys' individual interests; it affords opportunities for service and for leadership; and it is designed to retain the interest of Scouts throughout their five years' membership of the Troop.

THE LINK BADGE

Boys who enter the Troop as Cub Scouts coming up from the Pack, gain the Link Badge during their latter days with the Pack. Identical to the Scout Badge in its requirements, the Link Badge forms an essential part of the progressive training scheme, and lays emphasis on the unity of the training sections. It enables the Cub Scout to meet his future Scout Leader and, in addition, to take part in an outdoor Scouting activity with his future Patrol. Through his contact with that Patrol and with the Scout Leader, the gaining of the Link Badge ensures that the Cub Scout does not enter the Troop a stranger. This valuable feature should prove to be an important factor in minimising the loss to the Movement of boys at the transition period from the Cub Scout Pack to the Scout Troop.

THE SCOUT BADGE

Attainment of the Scout Badge is the basic requirement for membership of a Scout Troop. The aim should be for every new entrant to qualify quickly for full membership of the Troop by gaining the badge very soon after joining.

The requirements are purposely simple. Yet they are designed to ensure that, in his early days with the Troop, every boy is armed with sufficient factual and practical knowledge to enable him to decide whether or not the Scout way of life is the life for him — a decision that he alone can make, but one that *must* be made with knowledge and not in ignorance of its implications.

How serious this all sounds: and so it is. But to the boy such seriousness comes unnaturally, and should be tempered with an element of fun and adventure to satisfy his desire to experience straight away the active Scouting that attracted him to join. It is for this reason that in gaining the Scout Badge the boy is given an opportunity of joining in a worthwhile outdoor activity with his Patrol.

Background — Knowledge of the Movement

Before a boy becomes a Scout it is reasonable to expect him to have some knowledge of the Movement he is joining, including the life of the Founder, the start of the Movement and the development of world-wide Scouting. He must be made aware of the fact that he is joining not merely one particular Troop, but that his membership will make him part of the biggest Youth Movement this country, and indeed the world, has ever known.

The simplest way for the boy to gain this knowledge is probably, to him, the least inviting! Through his school-work he often finds himself the reluctant victim of a system that, for his ultimate benefit, requires him to spend an increasing portion of his spare time reading. He seldom wishes or expects the same demand to be made by his Scout Troop. Better, then, for the Scout Leader to expect of him the minimum of private study and to supplement such study by presenting the required knowledge by such means as yarns to the Troop and the use of suitable films.

Practical Experience — Outdoor Activity

It matters little, perhaps, what form the boy's first outdoor Scouting activity may take — a hike, an afternoon stunt, an expedition or cycle ride to a place of interest, or any one of a hundred others — but it should be seen to be exciting and worthwhile by the new boy taking part. It should preferably be an activity involving the boy with the Patrol and Patrol Leader with whom he will eventually be placed. In this way he will the quicker begin to find his place among his fellows and more readily form the friendships that will lead to his acceptance as a member of the Patrol.

Commitment — Scout Promise and Law

By making the Scout Promise a boy voluntarily commits himself to the Scout way of life. He cannot truthfully make that Promise without having a clear understanding of its meaning, and this involves both knowledge and understanding of the Scout Law.

It is not enough for the boy to be word-perfect in reciting the Promise and Law since they will have no significance in his life if they are unintelligible to him. The responsibility for explaining the implications of the Promise and Law falls to the Scout Leader personally, and is of such importance that it should not be delegated to an Assistant. Here, the Scout Leader's concern must be to ensure that the boy understands what is expected of him as a Scout in accordance with his age and development.

Clearly the boy's understanding and knowledge will develop as he himself develops, and it is for this reason that he is expected to show a progressive understanding of the Promise and Law at various subsequent stages of his training.

The Scout Leader's Part

It is vital for the Scout Leader to take a personal interest in the individual progress of each Scout in his Troop. His continuing encouragement, his friendship and his personal example are key factors in fostering and maintaining among his Scouts the enthusiasm for Scouting and the will to succeed that help to make his Troop a really going concern.

THE SCOUT STANDARD

The second stage in the Scout Progress Scheme not only covers the basic skills of Scouting, including the fundamentals of camping, cooking and exploring, but also encourages the Scout in his personal hobbies and interests. It should be possible for most Scouts to gain the Scout Standard within a year of joining the Troop.

At this stage all the badge requirements are obligatory, and rightly so, for only in this way is it possible to ensure that all Scouts reach a recognised standard of basic training compared with essential practical experience in the subjects they will meet at a more advanced level in subsequent stages of their progress.

A novel feature of the Scout Standard is that the Scout is required to satisfy not his Scout Leader but his own or another Patrol Leader of his ability to pass each of the requirements. Some may question the wisdom of placing this responsibility on Patrol Leaders; others may doubt the practicability of maintaining a set standard within the Troop. Experience shows, however, that boys can readily accept this degree of responsibility, and are sometimes so conscious of it that the standards they demand are higher than those that would be acceptable to the Scout Leader.

Our concern, then, must be to ensure that the standards we and our Patrol Leaders aim for are compatible with the particular ability of the individual Scout. Otherwise our eagerness to give real responsibility to our Patrol Leaders could act against the interests of the slower Scouts, quickly killing their enthusiasm and leading them to despair.

To place on the Patrol Leader the responsibility for examining Scouts for the Scout Standard tends to put him a little apart from his Patrol. This can have the desirable effect of strengthening his position as a key man in the structure of the Troop. But it demands that the Patrol Leader himself is thoroughly versed in the wide range of knowledge and skills required!

Notice, however, that all the subjects are well within the instructional ability of the trained Patrol Leader, and are admirably suited for use as the basis of a progressive series of Patrol Meetings and activities.

The Scout Leader's Part

The principles on which the requirements of the Scout Standard are based rely for their success on the Patrol Leader both "knowing his stuff" and having the ability to organise and carry through a progressive scheme of training and activity for his Scouts.

It is too much to expect the Patrol Leader to go it alone. He must be backed by a progressive system of training designed specifically to ensure that he possesses full technical knowledge in all the badge requirements, that he keeps ahead of his Scouts in their progress and that he is equipped to conduct attractive and worthwhile Patrol Meetings and activities.

As with many other aspects of Scouting in the Troop, the vital factor here is sound and continuing Patrol Leader training. The Scout Leader is primarily responsible for the conduct of that training, though his efforts may well be supplemented by the provision of Patrol Leader Training Courses at District level.

THE ADVANCED SCOUT STANDARD

Here the Scout is offered a series of opportunities for putting into practice the training he has received in his progress to the Scout Standard. In many subjects he is carried forward to further knowledge and higher skill, and throughout there is greater emphasis on doing than on merely knowing, for the requirements are essentially practical in content.

The Scout Leader should aim at getting *every* Scout to the Advanced Scout Standard, and, for most boys, this should normally be achieved before they reach the age of 14 years.

Although each group of requirements — self-reliance, service, adventure, Scoutcraft — retains an obligatory element, the Advanced Scout Standard introduces into the training scheme for the first time an element of choice. This exciting choice of purposeful activities allows the Scout some scope in planning his own progress through the scheme in the way that best suits his personality and his particular interests. However, the badge requirements are such that the Scout's choice of activity in one field or another will inevitably involve him in acquiring some new skill or fresh knowledge, for it is unlikely that he will have tried every one of them before.

The Scout Leader's Part

Many of the requirements of the Advanced Scout Standard provide tailor-made activities for inclusion as training sessions and activities at Troop Meetings and camps.

Certainly the intention is that the Scout should have the opportunity of choosing the particular features that appeal to him, but he cannot be expected to progress very far unless opportunities for training and practice are also provided. By including in his Troop programmes the activities suggested by the Scout Progress Scheme at all levels, the Scout Leader can ensure that the Troop is presented with a varied yet balanced field of activity, and in many cases he may awaken in his Scouts lasting interests in subjects that previously they had not thought of or had the courage to try.

THE CHIEF SCOUT'S AWARD

The Scout who gains the Chief Scout's Award sets the seal on his successful completion of the training provided in the Scout Troop. The Chief Scout's Award, the ultimate training award of the Scout Section, is entirely different in concept from any other Scout badge or any badge of any other Organisation.

The requirements for this Award are designed to encourage Scouts to reach high standards of personal achievement in a wide range of activities, to prove their worth by extending their qualities of responsibility and leadership, and to carry out responsible and worthwhile service to others.

Aimed primarily at the older boy, an essential feature of the Award is its self-programming approach. Within certain defined fields, there is a very wide choice of practical, purposeful activities that are sufficiently broad in scope to appeal to boys of all types, from "young gladiators" to quiet intellectuals. Like the Advanced Scout Standard, the accent throughout is on positive action, for mere theoretical knowledge in the absence of practical ability has no place in the Chief Scout's Award.

In the early stages of the Award the Scout is required to accomplish set standards in a variety of skills and practices, completing his own record of the date and place of each achievement. Here is a practical exposition of the first Scout Law, as well as positive recognition of the boy's achievements both within and outside the Troop.

Later he is required to pass on some of the training he has received in the Troop to other members of his Patrol, and to show himself willing and able to use his training in the service of others.

The Scout Leader's Part

In the past the Scout Leader has generally been regarded as

the expert in all the activities included in the training scheme — able to turn his hand to all things and to give his Scouts adequate practical instruction in all activities.

It is clearly unreasonable to expect any one man to possess technical ability in all the subjects covered by the Scout Progress Scheme, and, more particularly, in the many specialised activities required for the "Achievement" section of the Chief Scout's Award. Rather must he know where his Scouts can obtain instruction and practice in their preferred pursuits. He must be in possession of complete, up-to-date information on specialist instruction courses by such bodies as the District Scout Council, the local Youth Office and the C.C.P.R. For some specialist activities his Scouts will, in time, have at their disposal the Movement's own Activity Centres.

This is not to imply that the Scout Leader can take no active part in Scout training at Chief Scout's Award level. There is much to be done, and clearly many of the requirements lend themselves ideally to special projects for the older boys, while many others can be used as the basis of training sessions for the whole Troop. These may be conducted by the Scouters alone or in collaboration with friends of the Troop who are able and willing to act as occasional Instructors.

THE DUKE OF EDINBURGH'S AWARD SCHEME

In addition to taking part in the Scout Progress Scheme a Scout can participate in the Duke of Edinburgh's Award. There is much to commend this and details as to how this scheme operates can be found in Chapter 23 — Duke of Edinburgh's Award.

Chapter 9

THE PROFICIENCY SCHEME

The general scheme of training in the Scout Troop covers a very wide range of subjects — many of which require progressively higher standards of skill and knowledge at various stages of the scheme. It is clearly impracticable, however, for the scheme to embrace every subject in which boys of Scout age may find an interest, or to give training in all subjects to the highest standard that a boy may be capable of reaching.

For some boys, the training offered by the Scout Progress Scheme is all that they can reasonably assimilate in their time with the Troop. Others are well able to cope both with their normal Scout training and with additional interests and pursuits that are not specifically catered for in the general training scheme. Many more find their interest in some subjects awakened by their Scout training and wish to pursue that interest by acquiring more knowledge or skill than the Scout Progress Scheme requires.

The Proficiency Scheme is designed to cater for these individual tastes by providing, separately from the Progress Scheme but within the framework of the Troop, incentives for progressing along the lines suggested by the Scouts' particular interests and abilities. Properly used, the scheme provides a valuable adjunct to the general pattern of training offered in the Scout Troop, not only by encouraging Scouts to make good use of their leisure time but also by promoting a generally higher and broader-based standard of Scouting and by leading them on to high standards of achievement relative to their age and capability.

Scouts may enter for proficiency badges at any stage in their Scout training. Some badges are clearly intended for the young Scout, while others are designed to meet the needs of boys who have reached a fairly advanced stage of Scout training. But age alone should provide no bar to the Scout's entry for a particular badge — the important factors are his interest in the subject, the effort that acquiring the badge demands of him, and his ability to satisfy the badge requirements. The badges are so grouped, however, and the requirements so drafted that boys normally tend to enter for the particular types of badges that are best suited to their age and development.

CATEGORIES OF BADGES

There are four categories of proficiency badges, each of which is aimed primarily at a different level of attainment and at Scouts of different ages and different stages of development.

Interest Badges

The first group contains a limited number of badges, fifteen in all, that are designed to appeal to the younger Scout. The subjects covered are generally those in which young boys may find a passing interest or which may attract them as hobbies requiring only an elementary standard of skill. For these badges the requirements are simple and straightforward, and in most cases the knowledge necessary can be acquired readily in the normal practice of the particular subject. Entry for the badge can often have the desirable effect of co-ordinating the Scout's thoughts and actions in a purposeful direction.

Pursuit Badges

Aimed generally at Scouts of 13 to 14 years of age, Pursuit Badges form the main stream of the proficiency scheme. The requirements are intended to extend the boy's knowledge and skill in Sport, Technical and Scoutcraft subjects, his interest in many of which may follow the training he has received under the Scout Progress Scheme. The standard required for Pursuit Badges is generally higher than for the individual parts of the Chief Scout's Award in the particular pursuit concerned. In certain subjects, entry for a Pursuit Badge may be concurrent with the Scout's progress in the general training scheme, the gaining of the badge being acceptable as qualification in that subject in the Scout Progress Scheme. There are twenty-eight Pursuit Badges.

Service Badges

To encourage older Scouts in carrying out worthwhile forms of service both to the Movement and to the public, this special group of eleven practical badges has been devised. In the requirements for the badges, emphasis is laid on carrying out actual service using the knowledge acquired in gaining the badge. Service badges are particularly suitable for Scouts of 14 years of age and above, and, where appropriate, the requirements are in line with the recognised standards of specialist bodies outside the Movement.

Instructor Badges

This group of badges carries forward the principle of service to the Movement by offering Scouts opportunities for qualifying as instructors in subjects that are within the teaching ability of boys of 14 to 16 years of age.

Each badge requires a high standard in its particular subject, and in his progress towards gaining the badge the Scout must be given instruction in training methods and is expected to use the skill he has acquired by undertaking the training of other Scouts in that skill.

The subjects covered by the fifteen Instructor Badges are those in which young men of up to 16 years of age are capable of reaching such advanced standards of knowledge and experience that the instruction they give to younger members of the Troop can be expected to be thorough, practical and worthwhile.

It is important to note, however, that none of the subjects involves the degree of personal risk demanded by such pursuits as rock-climbing or mountaineering, for it would clearly be wrong to expect the candidate for an Instructor Badge to assume direct responsibility for the safety of Scouts under instruction in pursuits of this nature; and wrong to expose the Scouts themselves to anyone but an acknowledged specialist in such pursuits.

BADGE REQUIREMENTS

The individual requirements for all proficiency badges are given in full in a supplement to the publication *Policy, Organisation and Rules*. The following general notes, however, serve as a useful guide to the typical make-up of badge requirements and show the distinctions between the four groups.

Interest Badges — typical requirements

- elementary theoretical and practical knowledge of the subject.
- reasonable knowledge of materials, tools or other appropriate equipment.
- simple demonstration of practical ability in the subject at the time of examination.

Pursuit Badges — typical requirements

- good working knowledge of the use and maintenance of appropriate equipment.
- understanding of safety precautions if appropriate.
- sound ability in a reasonably comprehensive range of practical aspects of the subject.
- where appropriate, demonstration of skill in collaboration with other Scouts.

Service Badges — typical requirements

- demonstration of high standard of practical ability in the subject.
- use of practical ability in the service of the Movement or community over a period of time.

Instructor Badges — typical requirements

- hold the proficiency badge in the same subject.
- attendance at recognised course of training in technical skills and training methods.
- good working knowledge of basic principles of the particular skill, including good knowledge and understanding of safety precautions where appropriate.

- demonstration of practical ability at a more advanced level than that required for the corresponding proficiency badge.
- assist with the training of Scouts in the subject over a period of at least 3 months.

STANDARDS OF QUALIFICATION

It is impractical to assume that in every case the holder of a proficiency badge is an expert in the particular subject covered by the badge. It is, nevertheless, important that the standard of knowledge he possesses should be in accordance with his age and capabilities, and there is no merit in awarding a badge to a candidate who, by lack of sufficient effort or through reasons of age and development, cannot meet the requirements.

For badges in the Interest group it is usually unnecessary to define fixed standards. The prime purpose of these badges is to encourage progress on sound lines and clearly the Scouts who enter for them will have reached varying stages of advancement and skill. What is important is that the standard demanded should involve some effort on the part of the individual boy in order that he may sense real achievement in gaining the badge and feel encouraged to proceed further with his interest. To pitch the standard impossibly high defeats the object of the badge and could, in some cases, kill the boy's enthusiasm for his subject or deter him from attempting other badges at later stages of his Scout training.

Pursuit badges require the Scout to show a more definite standard of technical knowledge or skill, but in assessing the boy's achievement there must be some latitude to cater for individual circumstances. Among the factors that should be taken into account are the Scout's age and standard of intelligence, the effort he has applied in working for the badge, and the opportunity he has had of gaining practical experience. More difficult to assess than these factors, but nevertheless an important consideration, is the Scout's genuine interest in the subject covered by the badge — there is little point in him gaining the badge unless his interest in it extends to a real desire to make use of the knowledge he has acquired.

For badges in the Service section the conditions must be

strictly adhered to, for it is highly important that the Scout's knowledge of any subject in this group should be practical and thorough. A major feature of badges in the Service group is the requirement of actual service to the Movement or to the public. Such service cannot properly be carried out unless the Scout is fully competent in all the badge requirements, and it is right to expect high standards from the holder of this type of badge.

Similarly, a high level of attainment must be expected from Scouts who enter for Instructor badges. Here the requirement is for thorough, practical knowledge of the subject coupled with the ability and desire to instruct other Scouts to a reasonably high standard. Instructor badges are primarily intended for the older Scout who wishes to specialise in a particular subject, and the standard is such that, if effective and worthwhile use is to be made of the candidate in carrying out his instructional role, it is unreasonable to expect any young man to qualify for more than two badges in the group.

BADGE INSTRUCTION

Certain badges in each of the four groups cover typical Scoutcraft pursuits. For these subjects the necessary instruction can usefully form part of the Troop's normal programme.

Instruction in the subjects covered by some other badges may demand technical knowledge for which the services of lay Instructors may be required. Such Instructors can sometimes be found among the parents or friends of Scouts in the Troop, or may form part of a panel of Instructors recruited by the District Scout Council. As a means of using the services of Instructors to the best advantage it is usually advisable to form small special instruction groups composed of Scouts with like interests — either from Scouts in the same Troop, or from Scouts drawn from several Troops in the District.

For subjects involving advanced specialist knowledge or the use of special equipment or facilities that cannot be provided within the Scout framework, sometimes the best service the Scout Leader can give the Scout is to put him in touch with and help him to join a local club or other Organisation that specialises in the subject. For example, Scouts who are interested in specialising in photography would find their interests well-served by a photographic club, while those who are keen on marksmanship could obtain the practice they require as members of the junior section of a rifle club.

Whenever the services of outside Instructors are used in the training of Scouts, it is of prime importance that such Instructors are fully acquainted with the conditions and purpose of the badge for which their instruction is intended. In this way they can plan their instruction to cover the badge requirements fully to the set standard and can include such further instruction as the Scouts may require or be capable of accepting. It is not enough that their pupils should be presented merely with sufficient information and practice to gain the badge. Rather should the aim of the Instructor be to arouse such interest in the subject that the Scouts are encouraged to progress eventually to a more advanced standard of attainment than the badge demands.

EXAMINATION

Proficiency badges in the Pursuit, Service and Instructor groups are awarded by the District Scout Council on the recommendation of an independent Examiner — one of a panel of recognised Examiners appointed by the District Scout Council. The Scouter Leader is, however, responsible for arranging for the examination of his Scouts in the Interest group of proficiency badges. District Scout Councils can, of course, help the Scout Leader in this.

Before a Scout presents himself for examination in any proficiency badge, the Scout Leader should ensure that the Scout has reached a sufficiently high standard for a reasonable expectation of success. It is clearly discourteous to the Examiner, and a waste of his time, to expect him to deal with Scouts who are ill-prepared to meet the badge requirements.

The boy himself must have a full appreciation of the scope of the test and must be briefed in whatever conditions apply locally for its conduct. This, too, is the Scout Leader's responsibility.

Having satisfied himself on these important preliminaries, the Scout Leader should arrange for the Scout to enter for the badge at the earliest opportunity. The actual procedure to be adopted for making badge examination arrangements is largely a matter of District organisation, and the Scout Leader should acquaint himself with the particular procedure that applies locally. In some Districts it is left to the Scout Leader to make arrangements with the Examiner through the Badge Secretary, taking into account the Scout's most convenient times for examination. Having booked a suitable date and time, the Scout Leader informs the Scout of the arrangement and ensures that the boy is given the necessary form for signature by the Examiner after the examination.

There is, however, great merit in the system adopted in certain Districts, where the Scout himself contacts the Examiner and makes his own arrangements. This system can form a useful, albeit small, part of the Scout's general training by presenting him with a situation in which he is required to negotiate with a stranger — an easy matter for most boys, perhaps; but for some an ordeal than can be lessened by repetition and practice on occasions such as this.

Whatever method is adopted locally, the most important considerations are that the Scout, when ready to enter for the badge, should be allowed to do so with the least practicable delay; and having satisfied the Examiner should not be kept waiting for the presentation of the badge. Delays in the procedure before or after testing can only result in the serious disappointment of the Scout who has worked hard to qualify and may discourage him from attempting other proficiency badges. Much depends on co-operation and good liaison between Scout Leaders, Badge Examiners and the Badge Secretary.

Chapter 10

PROGRAMMES

Scout training is based largely upon programmes at Scout Meetings and the content and presentation of these programmes are consequently of first importance to both the Scout Leader and his Scouts. What a boy does at Scout Meetings is all-important to him; whether he enjoys them is the criterion by which he judges Scouting and his Leaders.

THE INTENTION

Programme material — on Troop Night, at week-ends, or at any other time — should be well thought out, attractive, interesting and enjoyable, and it should contribute towards the Scout's spiritual, mental and physical progress. Scouting is the best in life. It should be of help to boys at different stages of development and Scout programmes have to cater for the older as well as the younger boy, appealing not only to the imagination of the young Scout — agog to do things and enjoy new experiences — but also to the older boy who seeks realistic adventure and opportunities for putting his Scouting knowledge into practice. This is especially true of Patrol Leaders who enjoy challenging situations as individuals in addition to their role of organising and training younger boys.

Troop programmes should be broadly based to bring to the younger adolescent the exciting developments of the modern world around them. The mysteries of the universe; the sources and uses of energy; the many timeless wonders that appeal to boys; all have their place in Scouting and programmes should not be limited in their variety or scope. Boys have little time for useless knotting games or meaningless tests; they like to do things and to do them to some purpose.

WHAT SCOUTS WANT

Scouts want to be active. Badge progress should assist them with Scouting skills, and programmes provide them with opportunities for applying their knowledge and extending their experience. Scouts want adventurous activities. Recent surveys show that camping and outdoor activities are by far the most popular pursuits and this fact must be recognised in Scout Troop programmes. Scouting must be seen by the boys to be practical, outdoor and purposeful. Cosy, cut-and-dried routine does not satisfy the eager questing boys who join Scouts to find "the fresh excitements of new adventures." Scouters must feel free to adopt many and varied ideas for Scout training requiring imagination and initiative.

FREE SCOPE ACTIVITIES

The scope is tremendous and virtually unlimited; we know boys are active, curious, fun-loving and imaginative. They enjoy being members of a gang and as they get older they want to try things out for themselves. Examples of free scope activities range from skin-diving to visiting an artist in his studio; from making a space chart to visiting the control centre of a railway station or airfield. It is all good Scouting and such activities provide excellent opportunities for Patrol Meetings.

SPECIALIST ACTIVITIES

A number of Troops (and Patrols) may wish to specialise in a particular activity or interest over a period. The normal result is an upsurge in enthusiasm not only in the activity concerned but in the membership of the Troop. Boys like to belong to a successful outfit and a Troop which has a specialist skill in something — almost anything — has a tremendous advantage. The chosen activity may be a sport or perhaps a technical pursuit and the success of the Troop football team is a common example. Another Troop may undertake geological expeditions

(there is one particular "tough" Troop which delights in going armed with geological hammers looking for specimens) or they may prefer radio communications, the links with "ham" operators, the technical knowledge required, the building and operation of the radio stations providing sources of fascination and interest to many boys. After a time the Patrol Leaders' Council should consider new themes which will interest the Troop and enlarge their experience.

PROGRAMME MATERIAL

The wide range of free scope activities and specialist activities provides abundant material for both Troop and Patrol Meetings. There is no place for unnecessary restrictions on programme content, for freedom and flexibility are important factors in the development of Scout training. It may be convenient to group a number of activities under headings as examples of the interests and activities which are capable of infinite variation and extension:

Outdoor Programme

camping	gliding	orienteering
backwoods cooking	pioneering	ski-ing
climbing	football	service projects (road survey)
canoeing	fishing	historic sites
archery	karting	sailing
hiking	pony-trekking	cycling
swimming	wide games	hill walking
skin-diving	night activities	others sports
rescue	expeditions	visit airfields,
rowing	ornithology	fire/police stations

(Also occasional visits of all kinds, e.g. diesel engine sheds, power stations, water works, docks, science museums, outdoor exhibitions.)

Indoor Programme

construct a compass	boxing/gymnastics/judo
canoe building	model making of *all* kinds
space chart	entertainment groups

use of simple tools

first-aid emergencies
life-saving
exhibitions
collecting
safety precautions for adventurous activities
visit a control tower
visit engine repair shed
morse/semaphore

visit to a mill or stables
make a windmill
make a map or population survey
talk by a public service officer
photography — take and print
make a Patrol camera
build a weather station
demonstration by local sportsmen
painting and sculpture
as Patrol projects

SCIENTIFIC AND TECHNICAL PROGRAMME

natural science (flora and fauna) (collections, visits, displays)
radio communications (make a radio set)
forestry and conservation

how a car works

heat engines (marine & aero)
geology (specimens of locality)
make an electric motor

archaeology

how to work with metal

meteorology (weather charts, rain gauges)
astrology (go to an observatory)
make an electronic beam
make a working model turbine

make a working jet engine

Note: Many of these programme ideas are suitable for both indoor and outdoor sessions as Troop or Patrol activities with training aids to improve presentation, e.g. taped talks, film strips, activity commentaries. After trying out these ideas, with variations, you will be able to devise programme ideas which appeal to your boys. Breed tropical fish, make a hot air balloon — and get it to work, make a weather vane for your H.Q., draw up flight schedules to far-away places, make a telephone system in the Troop Room or camp, make a clock, run a market garden, hold a coin collection (can be rewarding) or run an International night with each Patrol contributing food representing a country of their own choice.

TRAINING SCHEMES AND PROGRAMMES

(a) The Scout Progress Scheme itself provides a vital source of excellent programme ideas and themes eminently suitable for Patrol and Troop Meetings. The Scout Badge and Scout Standard lend themselves to Patrol activities. The Advanced Scout Standard is more practical and provides suitable material for demonstrations (in and out-of-doors), e.g. pressure cooking, cooking, compass and pioneering. The Chief Scout's Award gives splendid opportunities for adventurous activities, social interests and service projects.

(b) The Sea and Air Training schemes offer great scope for even wider and more interesting programmes ideas. The potential is vast and a glance at the supplementary training schemes suggests wonderful opportunities for widening horizons and introducing new and exciting interests to *all* Scouts. Examples include the principles of flight and of navigation, charts, lights, signals, models and meteorology which open up new vistas of knowledge. For the older boy the study of space itself, flying, gliding, rowing, sailing, and other skills inherent in the elements of air and water offer exciting challenges to the more advanced Scout. This is the stuff of adventure — and of Scouting!

(c) The Proficiency Scheme, too, provides plenty of background material for Scout programmes. The introduction of wider interests in the Scout Progress Scheme will generate greater interest in the proficiency scheme with its different levels of badges to appeal to both younger and older boys. A look down the list will suggest many ideas for programme items and themes.

SOME PRACTICAL POINTS

Do – keep a record of your programmes. They will be worth their weight in gold for future reference and variation.
- take every opportunity to use the Patrol System.
- try and get help from outside experts and instructors.
- remember to discuss programmes with the Patrol Leaders' Council, remember their limited experience.
- use your Assistant Scout Leaders to the full and take advantage of up-to-date training aids to stimulate interest.
- try "programme planning" (see over).

TRAINING AIDS

There are many ways in which programme material can be made more attractive to boys. Several obvious and simple forms of visual aid, as well as more sophisticated equipment such as tape recorders and projectors, can prove extremely useful to the Scout Leader. Examples include demonstration kits (personal first-aid kit), simulated plastic wounds, mouth-to-mouth resuscitation models, see-through polythene rucsacs already packed, pictures of cloud formations, sectional diagrams of a car or jet engine, air charts, large-scale plans and maps.

Working models can be used to explain a complex activity, e.g. a pioneering project, heat engine or a prototype model of a Troop weather station, will stimulate interest and understanding of a Troop or Patrol venture.

Care must be taken, however, not to substitute indoor imitations of the real thing. Scouting is *doing* rather than talking or looking unless in preparation for more practical and worthwhile activities to follow.

PROGRAMME PREPARATION

Wider interests, the world around us, new training schemes, sea and air activities, there is so much to offer boys of Scout age, so much to include in Scout programmes. Preparation is essential and it is the essence of good leadership to plan ahead and know where you and your Troop are going! Not only the contents of the programme but the presentation and balance of a series of programmes must be considered.

PROGRAMME PLANNING

It is quite possible to become submerged in a sea of ideas and only by deliberate planning can the best use be made of the limited time at our disposal. Rigid time-tables which would prove restrictive should be avoided by having an overall and flexible plan to ensure balanced and well designed programmes over a period. For instance, a main theme, or themes, for a session interspersed with outdoor schemes, visits to other Troops, badge nights and special events could be arranged to satisfy the wide range of interests and ages of your boys and permit the Scout Leader and Patrol Leader that freedom and flexibility which is essential to enjoyable Scouting. Plan ahead and plan big.

WHAT PLANNING MEANS

It means looking ahead, mapping out the future and arranging your programmes in anticipation of the event. The advantages are obvious; your programmes are more attractive, more flexible and you can enlist expert help to make the best use of available time. Your Assistant Scout Leaders as well as the Patrol Leaders' Council should be consulted and even if this can only be done at the expense of some Troop time it is absolutely essential. Programmes over a period of, say, three months should include a balance of the following:

Patrol activities and outings
Outdoor and adventure activities
Special interests for Patrol Leaders and older boys
Opportunities for individual progress
New interests
Events involving outside relationships.

The key to successful programme planning lies in the ability of the Scout Leader to introduce a range of realistic, interesting and practical activities.

TROOP MEETINGS

A partly organised programme allowing time for free scope activities is a practical way of tackling the normal weekly meeting. This flexible approach should result in at least one-third of programme time taken over a period being available for wider interests (though not of *each* meeting); indeed, it may be better to devote a whole evening to a single worth-while activity than carve it up piecemeal with all the consequent time-wasting involved. 101 things just cannot be fitted into one short programme and the idea of novelties and gimmicks can be overdone in an attempt to meet the tastes of every boy. Planning over a period is essential to avoid the dangers of stereotyped programmes which eventually produce dull Scouters and dull Scouts. Programmes must have 'go' and be relevant to the needs of modern boys. *Activity* is the key-word.

PROGRAMME NOTES:

Flagbreak, for example, should whenever it is included be brief and its purpose clearly understood. Never an old flag hanging from a rusty nail by suspect sisal!

Inspections are hardly necessary every week and the Patrol Leaders' Council should consider carefully whether they are a routine requirement. They should always be short and snappy.

Subscriptions should be collected before, after or between Troop Meetings, or on a monthly or quarterly basis, but never during Troop or Patrol time. Subs. are the Patrol Leaders' responsibility.

Prayers at the end of a meeting are certainly desirable provided they are suitable and sincere. The Patrol Leader should be brought in and the responsibility shared. A theme for the session basea on *A Plain Man's Book of Prayers* or *Prayers for Use in the Brotherhood of Scouts* is effective and avoids last-minute uncertainty. Boys' own prayers can be most moving.

Notices should and must be kept brief. Sometimes Scouters talk too much; never keep boys standing unnecessarily, it is discourteous and indicates poor leadership. Written notices can often be given at a convenient moment during the meeting.

Patrol Corners are often sadly misused; they become periods of suspended animation and in consequence achieve very little. The term "Patrol Time" is a better expression, implying opportunities for activity and progress. It is not sufficient for the Scout Leader merely to abdicate in favour of the Patrol Leader for the odd half-hour. Patrol time must be used to advantage and programme planning is again required as there should be a plan of action. The Patrol Leaders are briefed, or they brief the Scouters, on what they intend to do with their boys — all of them — the older and the younger members. The older boys, for instance, may be taking instruction from an outside expert while the Patrol Leader takes the younger lads through their Scout Standard. Patrol time is the Patrol System in action, but give the Patrol Leaders guidance, don't just leave them to it!

Games have their place, especially for fun and also for training. They are good warmers-up, while rough games and sense training exercises can, if not overplayed, provide breaks, or links, in the general programme. They are not just time-fillers — otherwise the cry goes up at home and at school — "We don't do anything worthwhile at Scouts." This is the arch villain behind leakage and more boys leave Scouts for this reason than all others put together.

OUTDOOR MEETINGS

At least one meeting a month all the year round (but more in Summer) should be out of doors. The Scout Progress Scheme is largely outdoor in content and there is terrific scope for sports, camping, hiking, wide games and adventure activities. Sufficient excuse for outdoor meetings every week ! Separate chapters refer to outdoor and adventure activities which can be mounted on either a Troop or Patrol basis. Training in safety precautions is very important and can itself provide good programme material with an outdoor and adventurous flavour.

PATROL MEETINGS

The Patrol is the basic unit of Scouting; it is essential to the success of Scout training and Scout programmes. Some Troops hold regular weekly Patrol Meetings, with only infrequent meetings of the full Troop on formal occasions. Adequate notice must be given to the Patrol, who should be free to plan their own particular programmes. The Scout Leader needs to know what is prepared and be ready to give guidance or help with the realisation of their plans. Later he should show interest in the Patrol's endeavours, and ensure that the meetings have not been aimless or a waste of time. The Patrol Leaders' Council is the proper medium for discussing future plans and enabling the Patrol Leaders to share ideas and experiences. Suitable activities include: hiking with a special purpose, visits to places of interest, social service training in special skills, and the development of Patrol interests such as crafts and cooking. Ideas should be discussed and action planned by the whole Patrol in Council. This type of activity is Scouting at its best.

WEEK-END MEETINGS

Week-end Scouting is the real thing; the time when training is put into practice, the time for enjoying Scouting to the full without the limitations of short evenings and homework. Boys cannot be trained on one night a week and nothing more. Frequent day, half-day and week-end meetings for the Troop or a Patrol provide the taste of adventure which is missing from Troop Night. These activities can often be led by an Assistant Scout Leader or the Patrol Leader himself.

Reference has already been made to outdoor and adventure activities and the scope is enormous. Full use should be made of District and County facilities (which should become increasingly available) and there are often opportunities for Troops to combine, particularly in providing Leaders and with transport arrangements. Activity bases and adventure centres are to be encouraged, and supported. This type of Scout meeting really appeals to boys.

The list of activities on pages 87/88 can easily be extended and adapted to meet the needs of the locality and the interests of the particular Troop. Scouting should provide youngsters with a passport to new and exciting pursuits and above all with opportunities to go camping. One Patrol camp or outing a month is a good target or, alternatively, a visit to a Scout or Youth Hostel in the Winter. Patrol Leader training and badge courses are also much more effective at week-ends and in view of other commitments it is advisable to give notice of week-end activities well in advance. Programme planning applies equally to week-ends and outdoor meetings if they are to be worthwhile, properly mounted and well attended.

PROGRAMME PLANNING IN ACTION (An Illustration)

Themes for the period — Map and Compass; Canoeing

Spend half a night on a worthwhile activity, e.g. a talk and practical demonstration (judo, photography, aircraft recognition, cooking a kabob, making and flying a kite).

An outdoor meeting by Patrols: meet at grid reference . . treasure hunt by compass bearings.

Progress Scheme meeting: mainly badge progress and 'Patrol time,' including taped commentary on a canoeing adventure with display of equipment.

*Week-end activity; canoeing for Patrol Leaders and Assistant Patrol Leaders.
Troop Night with outdoor visit to engine sheds by Patrols. Finish at H.Q with indoor sports or 'pop' and biscuits.
'Camp Night' indoors, slides of camp; outdoors, pitch tent in dark.
Planned wide games to include compass bearings and reciprocals (joint meeting with other Troop).
*Training session for Patrol Leaders and older boys on weather lore.
Patrol projects (allied to training schemes, e.g. pioneering, backwoods cooking).
*Visit to swimming baths for practice and demonstration of canoe paddling techniques.
Patrol week-end with archaeological flavour.
Visit by Troop or Patrol to County Adventure Centre.

The variations are legion!

*These events are for Patrol Leaders and older boys who have attained Advanced Scout Standard.

PROGRAMME PLANNING OF CAMP

A good camp is well planned and assured of success before the boys leave home. No rigid schedule is needed although an outline programme is required with careful thought given to practical ideas capable of execution at the camp itself. These ideas can be adapted according to the progress of the camp. the weather, and other opportunities which may arise for providing good programme material. A theme or special activity based on local knowledge can contribute greatly to a successful and enjoyable camp, and what better opportunity is there for trying something different or unusual than in the free and flexible environment of a Scout camp? It is worth noting that long notice not only results in good attendance but also discourages boys from leaving the Troop or losing interest when they know there is an attractive camp to an exciting place in the offing.

OTHER MEETINGS

Special events and unusual meetings can boost morale as well as create interest and enthusiasm. Patrol exhibition, Troop demonstrations, joint meetings, trophy night, banquets, theatre or cinema outings add point and enjoyment to a series of programmes. They also encourage parental interest and the support of other interested persons and can be a means of finding supporters and instructors.

Exchange visits with other Troops (or their Patrol Leaders) will help to broaden the outlook of your Scouts, particularly if the boys are from different localities.

MIXED ACTIVITIES

We sometimes tend to be shy of boy and girl activities although many successful schemes have been carried out in different parts of the country. Is there a place for this in your plan? These activities often take place in conjunction with a Guide Company but they can, of course, include other Organisations, especially if planned for the benefit of the older boys. Mixed activities are usually for training or social purposes and joint training courses for Scout/Guide Patrol Leaders have proved very successful. Girls often surprise boys with their agility and their quick understanding of new skills. The boys frequently surprise everybody by their marked improvement in dress and appearance! These activities require careful planning as well as the enthusiastic co-operation of the Patrol Leaders' Councils concerned, but where there are competent section leaders willing to have a go there is plenty of scope for such ventures. Life is, after all — a joint adventure.

A NEW DIMENSION

Programmes which are enjoyable appeal to boys; where they are relevant to their needs and have the freedom and flexibility inherent in the Scout method, the result will be attractive and successful Scouting. The aims of the section can only be achieved and individual progress be made through the deliberate use of the Patrol System in activities and badge training schemes. Where programmes are based on the Scout Promise and Law and the Scouters by their example convey the spirit of Scouting, then a new dimension will become apparent — one of lasting depth as well as breadth in the training of their Scouts.

Chapter 11

WEEKLY MEETINGS

Although a Scout ought to spend about three hundred of his waking hours each year at camp, and probably only about one hundred at weekly Troop Meetings, the latter will inevitably loom large in his view of Scouting. So the weekly meetings have got to be good — indeed such that the Scouts would not miss them for anything. An impossible target, perhaps, but we must try.

The boy joins the Movement because he wants to have fun in the company of his friends. But this does not mean unlimited freedom for messing about: he wants to be organised, and he hates it when he is not. He wants new fun; we must try to give him up-to-date fun. But this does not mean we are scrapping all the old ideas; most of the original recipes for Scouting were, and still are, excellent.

The boy joins us because he wants to 'belong' — to a respectable gang. So we must use the Patrol System whenever possible or suitable. It has been found to be by far the best way of organising nearly every Scout activity for boys of the ages with which we are dealing.

The Scouts want, indeed need, a stable, reliable basis for their Scouting. This means our meetings must always start on time, with the Scout Leaders there, the Patrol Leaders there, the Scouts there, and the programme there. Meetings normally start with flag-break and inspection, and end with flag-down and prayers; but inspection, for instance should not take more than a couple of minutes. Although it may be contrary to his normal inclinations, the boy respects a small amount of discipline. So don't be shy of giving orders; the boys expect to be told to 'fall in,' 'alert,' 'easy,' 'break off,' and they won't respect you if you shirk giving orders. Some Scouters, like inexperienced school-teachers, are scared of being unpopular, and do not realise that firm discipline *is* popular. Scout Leaders must also watch the Patrols in this matter. The Patrol Leaders need even more help, and must have the Scouters' support in checking any rebellion.

Boys joining Scouting know that it consists of learning things and passing tests, and they want this. They want to make progress, and they want to explore new fields of interest. They also thoroughly enjoy competition, and it is good for them. They should be encouraged to compete, individually and as Patrols, as often as possible. Furthermore, although we don't want to encourage boastfulness, boys like to advertise their achievements, and wear the badges they have won. B.-P. understood this bit of psychology when he devised the badge system.

It is, of course, absolutely essential to plan beforehand what you are going to do at a Troop Meeting. This planning must include the details of the particular evening, as well as the general plan for a whole series of meetings. It is a very good idea to prepare your training syllabus for a period of three months — for the whole year, if possible. One way is to plan meetings in three groups of about fourteen weeks, roughly corresponding to school terms. Most Troops are not school Troops, but inevitably you will have some sort of break at Christmas, with a party, a theatre visit, perhaps, and a good turn. At Easter there will be a break, with a training camp for 13, 14 and 15-year olds, and in August there will be a break for Summer camp and family holidays.

Be prepared to change the programme if there is a good reason, but unless the plan is found to be definitely bad, don't change it too easily — this would undermine the boys' confidence in the planned programme. There should, however, be surprise items. Put the word 'mystery' on the advertised programme, if you can be sure it will be good, and the Scouts will look forward to the next one.

WEEKLY MEETINGS

The following Autumn instruction programme was devised for a school Troop which met from 4.0 p.m. to 6.0 p.m. — so they had daylight for the first six weeks. They had a grass area available quite near their Headquarters, and it was not too difficult to 'get into the country' by bus. This particular programme, as it stands, is obviously not suited to every Troop, but it shows the sort of planning which must be done, and suggests how we can get plenty of interesting variety without straying too far from the subjects and tests of the training scheme. Details of the interval games are not shown — indeed, they were not decided very far ahead, and were sometimes varied according to the mood of the boys, or the weather. As bad weather training alternatives, we were ready to bring forward at short notice some of the first-aid sessions; and also in reserve we had a 'bingo' session (see P. 102), and some items aimed at improving hike logs — help in sketching, drawing maps, etc.
(YS = young Scouts — 1st and 2nd year)
(OS = older Scouts — usually 3rd and 4th year).

Week 1:

(a) YS Hike Tents } Instruction and practice in pitching and
OS Itisa Tents } striking and folding.
(b) A showing of the film of Summer Camp.

Week 2:

A Map-reading exercise, — going out by bus, then hiking in groups of three, a distance of about 1½ miles, meeting Scout Leaders or Venture Scouts at several points, having to answer questions which tested how far they had compared observation of the map and the land.

Week 3:

(a) YS Study pictures teaching about fires and fire-places. + Axe rules — short revision by a Scout Leader.
OS Pressure Stoves — how to light them and look after them, including the snags.
(b) Knots for joining ends together — revision by Patrol Leaders.

Week 4:

(a) YS Bends and Hitches — taught by a Scout Leader.

Packing a rucsac — discussed with another Scout Leader.
OS Preparing pioneering using bends and hitches.

(b) Patrols under Patrol Leaders tried out the 'Liverpool' Transporter, which requires correct use of clove hitches and rolling hitches, and good control by Patrol Leader.

Week 5:

'Hike Camps' — Within the 1½ hours available, Scouts in twos or threes have to pitch a hike tent, light a fire, cook a simple dish and make a hot drink, strike and pack the tent, and wash up utensils. The younger Scouts used 'Gilwell' hike tents, and wood fires; the Patrol Leaders and Assistant Patrol Leaders had 'Itisa' tents and pressure stoves. Five or six aspects were inspected and marked for competition purposes.

Week 6:

'Venture Trail' — A short stroll in Patrols, practising map-reading, and encountering two simple 'incidents.'

Week 7:

(a) Loops and Bights — taught by Patrol Leaders; followed by an activity involving practice at various ways of lifting and lowering people on ropes.

(b) Rehearsal of demonstration for Parents' Evening.

Week 8:

Parents' Evening.

Week 9:

A Wide Game — on a local heath.

Week 10:

(a) YS Personal first-aid kits — combined with further revision of last week's first-aid.
OS Troop first-aid kit, and Camp health.

(b) Clouds, winds and weather.

Week 11:

(a) YS Cuts, stings, burns, fainting;
OS Bleeding, shock, sprains, fractures.
Revision sessions really.

(b) Local knowledge scavenger hunt.

Week 12:

'Resuscianne' model — for Mouth-to-mouth resuscitation drill — borrowed from local St. John Ambulance. In order that all Patrols should be able to practise, they rotate through various other activities, including gas and fire emergency teaching, and some test passing.

Week 13:

Simulated accidents — each Patrol to deal with two, and have thorough 'post mortem' and teaching on each.

All the subjects of the Scout training scheme, and a great deal else that is useful and interesting, can be included in your meetings. Indeed, you *must* cover the whole of the training scheme at least once in the course of a year. As far as possible, this should be done progressively, and opportunities for passing the tests should be offered.

It is very desirable that the Patrol Leader should teach his Patrol wherever suitable, but it is sometimes better to have separate instruction groups for different ages. There are times when Scout Leaders can talk or demonstrate to the whole Troop; but this should not happen too much, and their part ought probably to be limited to five minutes, before the Patrols go and practise what was being demonstrated.

'Patrol Time' instruction or activity is very good training, both for the Scouts, and for the Patrol Leader; but it is essential to see that the Patrol Leader is properly briefed. It is wrong to assume that because he has done a particular activity three times before, he therefore knows how to run it, or how to teach it. We must go over each aspect in detail at the Patrol Leaders' Council.

It is a good idea for the Patrol Leaders' Council to be another weekly meeting, — to prepare for each week's Troop Meeting. it could, perhaps, be on a separate evening, or a Sunday afternoon tea party, or an extra half-hour after the Troop Meeting; or an extra long one could be held every fortnight, or once a month. But adequate preparation, of and by the Patrol Leader, must be made. He must know:—

exactly what and how he is going to demonstrate,

- which points he will emphasize,
- how he will get his Patrol to copy his demonstration,
- how he will test that the 'knowledge' has got across,
- what errors to look for and correct.

Consider, for instance, the simple square lashing: do your Patrol Leaders know that:–

- there are two right ways and at least six wrong ways of tying the initial clove hitch?
- the turns should be added outwards on one spar and inwards on the other? — and why?
- there are several wrong ways of starting the frapping turns?
- there are two right ways, and at least fourteen wrong ways of making the final clove hitch?
- and why?

Well, do *you* know?

Detailed preparation is well worth while. The boys will soon begin to appreciate your efforts (and will even sooner notice your lack of preparedness!). It may sometimes take 60 minutes to get ready a five-minute activity; but preserve all your notes and details for a repeat next year, and make a note of any faults or possible improvements in the scheme. We once organised a 'Bingo' session. Each Scout was given a card which had on it a dozen or twenty numbers, referring to questions. Scattered around the Troop Room were eight or ten Scouters and Venture Scouts, who asked the Scouts the questions. If they knew the answer, the Scouter initialled against the appropriate number; if they did not know, they could consult numerous books, cards, diagrams, etc., placed in the centre of the room. The numbers on the cards were suitably arranged so that the Patrol Leaders and older Scouts had to answer more advanced questions than the younger ones. The first Scout to finish probably shouted 'Bingo,' but we carried on until a fair number had finished. The preparation took more than two hours, but we stopped the game after half-an-hour. We have, however, preserved all the cards and question lists, so that we can rapidly produce the game another time.

In Patrol activities, the Patrols are going to be **doing** something, — possibly complicated, — possibly each Patrol different

So it is desirable that any instructions should be in writing. Write them on a post-card, so that they can be kept for the future. You might have four Patrols on four activities, which they take in turns for four weeks. Many ideas and schemes can be obtained from the Training Supplements of *The Scouter*.

Actual instruction in the technical details of Scouting is normally greatly helped if diagrams are available. Again, the various Scouting periodicals contain excellent examples which can be preserved pasted on card. The Scout Association has also published wall-charts. But why not draw your own, and have them photo-copied — such things as diagrams showing the correct stages in pitching a tent, or a blank local road-map, for details to be filled in? It might be a good idea to type and duplicate the correct treatment of a first-aid incident, so that after the Scouts have dealt with a 'patient,' they can check how well they did it; there might not be enough Scouters to watch and comment on each Patrol.

There is an increasingly large number of films becoming available, some of which can be borrowed free of charge. These can be used to educate in many Scouting skills, like the weather and mountaincraft, and also to stimulate interest in a much wider variety of subjects, such as the Police, or coal-mining, or the manufacture of meat-pies! In general, boys seem to get bored more rapidly with shows of 'still' pictures. (See Chapter 26 — on Training Aids).

We have found that Scouts are very keen on competitive 'incidents' which give them the challenge associated with a Venture Course. But these do not have to be of the athletic 'getting across the bottomless ravine' type. They can consist of simple things like pitching a hike-tent, lighting a primus, making a trestle, treating a cut leg, etc. Again it is probably best to put the instructions (and perhaps the solution) in writing. In many of these simpler activities, it may be better to split the Patrols, so that you have groups of three or four, instead of seven or eight. This allows twice as many Scouts to be actually doing something, — but it does mean you need twice as much equipment.

Finally among your preparations for a Troop Meeting should be a post-card with the whole evening's programme written on it. Again it should be filed away for future reference, with notes of things that could be improved next time. It is probably true to say that every programme can be improved next time, because we should be continually advancing with the times and keeping up-to-date. The last thing we would advocate is that we should use the same programme for the third week in October every year!

We must, indeed, introduce to our Scouts, a much wider range of activities than has been traditional. Go-ahead Troops have being doing this for some years, and we can all learn from their experience, and perhaps advance still further. But we must beware of three things:

- doing things which the boys already get elsewhere, i.e. things which schools or other specialist clubs do better;
- having *too many* 'extra mural' activities: most visits you would not want to repeat within four years, so you would need a fairly large repertoire to find even one for every three months;
- abandoning *Scouting*; boys join us for Scouting, and will leave us if they do not get it.

A visit to a place of interest can only replace the normal weekly evening meeting if it is very local. But such activities could be extras or variations during the school holidays or half-term holiday. Then there will be no competition with school home work, and there will be time to travel some distance.

Visits to the Troop by outside speakers on special subjects are an excellent idea, and can easily be fitted into the normal Troop Meeting framework. (Indeed the visitor might be keen to see some other Scouting activity before or after his bit.) Such visits could probably take place every four to six weeks without overdoing it. Or a short series of weekly talks by an expert on subjects relevant to Scouting, such as first-aid, weather, or firefighting, could be arranged. Try to make sure that your speakers do not 'lecture' for more than twenty minutes, unless they are:

- demonstrating, and getting the boys to practise,
- or are showing slides or films,
- or are answering questions,

- or (in very rare cases) they are really holding the boys enthralled.

Many of the 'newer' activities need much preparation of equipment, — or the Scouts themselves must be warned to bring it. For instance, in the electrical line, we might try:

- making a circuit for a two-way switching light;
- learning how to wire up a three-pin plug;
- making a morse buzzer, or a telephone circuit;
- making a radio.

Or in carpentry, given the tools and materials, the boys could make for the Troop: canoes, tables, stools, benches, display boards, etc. Photography, model-making, etc., are other possibilities, if you can obtain the necessary equipment. But with all of this type of activity, we must consider carefully whether we really want to try them within the normal weekly Troop Meetings. The more complicated and more specialist ones (a) may take several meetings to achieve any success, and (b) may not interest everyone, so you must have choices available in order to keep all the Scouts active. In fact, this will raise the question of whether you will need to open your Scout Headquarters on a different evening for specialist or hobbies activities. There is, however, always a case for introducing a practical demonstration by an expert, at one Troop Meeting, which might awaken the boys' interest in a new pursuit. We certainly want to widen the scope of our Scouts' activities, but we must equally certainly think very carefully about what is brought into the weekly Troop Meeting.

Games in Troop Meetings are really of three types:—

(a) those for letting off steam, (b) instructional and training games, (c) just mad, but fun.

Type (a) are very useful at the beginning of a meeting, — or better still, *before* the meeting. If the boys have spent a large proportion of the meeting sitting down, they could let off steam briefly just before the end. Sometimes, rough games need some careful organisation, because it is often not a good idea for 11-year-olds to be playing them with 15-year-olds.

Type (c) need not be totally excluded, but they should not be childish, and should rarely last more than five minutes or so.

Type (b) are very important to Scouting, because Scouting

is training, but it is also fun. It may often be difficult to distinguish between a competitive training activity and a training game; but they must be thought out carefully. In general, we must:

- beware of too many relays, where only one boy in six is actually doing anything,
- beware of racing activities which must be done properly; e.g. first-aid can rarely be taught by any sort of game;
- beware of too many knock-out games, where the less able (who need most practice) spend most of the time watching.

There is, of course, a fourth type of game — the 'Wide Game,' which would take all or most of a Troop Meeting. Having about three a year is probably enough, for presumably they will play others at camp. The variations on 'flag raiding,' 'coppers and robbers,' 'release-o,' etc., with a 'fighting' element, are only possible in parks or open country. In the interests of safety, street games must usually take the form of a 'treasure trail'; but these can be very good training value.

An evening devoted entirely to short games should be very rare. The annual Christmas party is probably enough, but it might be worth having such a programme up your sleeve, in case, for instance, a wide game has to be cancelled because of bad weather.

Boys join Scouting to have fun, but fun is not just fooling about, and although Scouting is a game, it is not continual children's games. It is probably sufficient to have an energetic game before the start, one or two training games in the middle, and a final quick game that is useless but fun, five minutes before notices and prayers.

The two Gilcraft books on *Indoor Games* and *Outdoor Games for Scouts* are excellent sources of ideas, and there are frequent suggestions in *The Scouter*. But in the end, your own wide experience will suffice, if you make a note of each good game you hear of, and also note possible improvements after you have tried it.

It is very usual to run a Patrol Competition at Troop Meetings. It undoubtedly helps to keep the Patrol Leaders on their toes, and, perhaps more important, it encourages the Scouts to back up their Patrol Leader. It is important to be *consistent* in:

- the way points are awarded,
- when points are awarded,
- what points are awarded for.

It often needs an Assistant Scout Leader with this as his special responsibility, but perhaps one of the Assistant Patrol Leaders can be appointed as recorder.

Normally, the points for one evening will hardly be enough for one period of the competition; it would be better to award the prize or trophy after a month or six weeks. It is best to have a tangible prize of some sort. One system is for the winning Patrol Leader to be presented with the trophy by the Patrol Leader who held it last. But alternatively, or also, there could be permanently held prizes such as books for the Patrol library.

Points would normally be awarded for attendance, promptness, smartness, competitive games and activities, and progress at test-passing. The last can cause complications, because somehow a careful record must be kept of who has passed what during the month. It is also usually argued that some tests are worth more than others, and a detailed scheme has to be devised.

Lastly, if it can be done surreptitiously, we must avoid letting one or two Patrols get so far behind that they give up trying, for then the object of the competition would be defeated. We are not so much trying to prove who is best, but trying to encourage the not-quite-so-good to get a little better.

All Troop Meetings will normally end with prayers. There are several books which give excellent advice and help on prayers for boys. We would just urge three things: first, that our prayers should be appropriate, — pray for Johnnie's mother who is ill, or for the harvest, or for the new Scout just invested. Secondly, that our prayers should be in simple language, which the boys can clearly understand, — so that they can indeed be praying themselves, and not just hearing someone else doing it. This leads thirdly to the suggestion that the boys themselves should read the prayers. Patrols may take it in turns, and it need not be the Patrol Leader; but don't let him simply 'pass the buck' to a young Scout who is not really sure of himself. Perhaps the most important aspect of Troop prayers is that the Scout Leader who is encouraging them should really believe that they matter. To this question of leading our boys to God, much thought must be given.

Indeed, in this whole matter of leading our boys, great care must be taken. It is astonishing, humbling, indeed frightening, how much our Scouts will copy us. The original 1908 Scouts invented Scoutmasters in order to legalise their mischief. But boys nowadays still want to know and to have personal contact with adults whom they can trust at all times to help them to enjoy life and to grow up the right way. It is at the Weekly Troop Meetings, nearly as much as at camp, that our Scouts will be learning from us how to live.

Chapter 12

OUTDOOR ACTIVITIES

The 'OUT' in Scouting has been preached for many years and most of us go through the motions. Too often in urban Troops this means once-round-the-block wide games or street lamp observation, all bound within the straight-jacket of the two-hour weekly meeting. B.-P.'s concept of adventure was more imaginative than that. Even the better Troops were in danger of extracting from his writings only the woodcraft elements by putting their noses to interminable nature trails or tying themselves up in the inconsequential expertise of pioneering projects. What it should mean is more substance in our activities, the opportunity to drink deep and much greater flexibility (particularly in time-tabling).

Unless you escape from the routine of 7 'till 9 on a Wednesday evening your programme can never be varied enough or worthwhile. Get away from the Headquarters. Arrange to meet miles away and get right on with a single activity like horse riding: it isn't essential to start every meeting with flag-break, inspection and notices under your own roof. Break the routine by extending a Friday night meeting to a midnight hike, camp, breakfast and bus back for a full Saturday. In this way you will not be competing directly with other worthwhile week-end activities. To add a pinch of adventure to your activities you should first develop a flexible attitude of mind, and to establish this attitude you must force yourself to vary your approach so that the dead hand of routine doesn't take the helm instead.

CAMPING

Dropping a routine doesn't mean dropping the technique of the past. The skills of camping and fire lighting and cooking must still come first. This is what the eleven-year-old wants to do most. Let him get right on with it from the night he joins.

We have tended to make a mystique of Scout camping. The skills are not so difficult that they require years of apprenticeship. All that is needed is opportunity, encouragement, practice and some sharing of knowledge. The Scout doesn't even need guidance from the rich fund of your woodcraft lore. A routine too rigid or a paragon too exalted might kill the adventure or chill the joy of the boy's first 'crispy' twist. This is not to say that you should be prepared to debase camping standards. Show a positive interest rather than a tight control and train your Patrol Leaders to aim high, but let the boy's first year be full of opportunity to make mistakes. It is your job to provide plenty of practice right from the beginning.

Next, extend the range of the equipment and the techniques involved in camping. Introduce cooking by pressure stoves, with menus based on dehydrated or accelerated freeze dried foods. Before the Christmas present season persuade a camping supplier to come and discuss the merits of various sleeping bags, anoraks and rucsacs. Above all, see that there are many opportunities for experiment under canvas. Most of these should be in conjunction with an outdoor activity; avoid theoretical exercises in tent erection, cooking on the waste ground behind the Headquarters. At a week-end where the older Scouts are rock-climbing there could be a Scout Standard group acting as camp staff in between their shorter introductory sessions on the rock face. Above all remember that you will not give a new recruit enough camping if you insist on being present on every occasion. Foster Patrol camping to the full. See that each Patrol has its own tentage and equipment, completely self-contained and independently maintained. This might only be possible if you move away from the concept of heavy, standing camp equipment. If your Patrol Leaders are young or inexperienced break down the prejudice against permanent camp sites; you will feel easier if they are camping there with help at hand. Make more use of indoor accommodation, for this will extend your season and provide as many valuable experiences as a camp.

CHOICE OF FURTHER ACTIVITY

Once you have laid firm foundations in self-reliant camping you will need to look wider in preparing your programme for the year. Some of your activities will need to be short, self-contained exercises, expeditions and wide games, but see that your programme isn't dominated by such isolated islands of interest. Aim to introduce a number of activities which provide continuity and depth, which require new skills to stretch both the new recruit and the Scout who has got to Advanced Scout Standard, and which offer wider horizons of interest and endeavour.

Even while planning a short exercise remember that modern youth is far more sophisticated than was his counterpart even ten years ago. Certainly camping, fire-lighting and cooking still appeal, but even enthusiasm for this will run out in a year if not used in different situations. You have to compete with gadget equipped 'special agents' rather than with buckskin frontiersmen. The shape and form of the wide game or hike as described in our Association's books is always valid, but see that the theme is really suitable to the modern mind. In the place of string 'electric' fences give Scouts an opportunity to use some of the machinery of modern living. There is no point in buying expensive equipment just to enliven a hike but if you would find a battery tape recorder essential for your major activity then buy it and use it imaginatively when planning hikes (recording ancient customs or local dialect).

If you are going to encourage your older Scouts in their pursuits you might use their skill with radio controlled models or cameras to make wide games more realistic. The recommended book list which appears from time to time in *The Scouter* will provide you with several titles full of hints on planning hikes and wide games: all that you have to do is to see that you are 'tuned in' to the uses of twentieth-century ironmongery.

MAJOR ACTIVITIES

When discussing with your Patrol Leaders the choice of a major activity for the season avoid the pitfall of believing that it must be gladiatorial or 'hearty.' Certainly it must be adventurous, but with enthusiastic leadership there can be as much adventure in archaeology or butterfly hunting as in mountaineering or pot-holing. The secret is in the leadership. Do not be ashamed of pointing the Troop in the direction of your own interest as long as the activity can be used as a means of passing on Scout skills. After all, you are the best form of continuity a Troop can have — much more valuable than the activity itself. If you have no strong interest avoid flitting about, tasting here and there, without ever getting to grips with real skills. By all means sample but don't leave your programme rootless.

Try to find one (or possibly more) activity which will take the interest of the whole Troop, an activity which will raise the need to acquire other skills (such as photography or mapping) and which will give a sound reason for more camping or hiking. This activity will then be a core of interest around which you can construct a wide programme. The list of proficiency badges — from angling to smallholding — should provide ideas for such activities. Even this core should not be thought of as immovable. It will change according to current taste or the specialist help you can recruit. But make sure you can do it well. It is better to engage in a less worthwhile project that you can do well than a more worthwhile one for which you lack the facilities.

If you have a team of good Patrol Leaders with very positive interests it might so happen that you will develop separate projects for each Patrol, each so different that they will tend to keep the Troop apart. This will not be harmful if these are real enthusiasms and you are able to provide the support needed by way of equipment and instructors. More often than not there will be no such positive lead and it will be necessary for you to infuse some enthusiasm into your Patrol Leaders and to fan the flames of a common interest. See that it is an activity which will cater for many skills. Very few skills as such will be apparent at first and it will be necessary to jolly certain boys into a job, but if you have made a sound choice of activity you will soon establish pride in the job.

Your jobs will vary according to the activity but might include Quartermaster, official Photographer, Secretary, Surveyor, Librarian, Transport Officer. Once you have provided Instructors to train your team, make sure that the skills are not lost. Establish a system of inherited responsibility. The official Photographer should have a younger deputy and possibly a recruit apprentice. Each is responsible for training his successor so that movement of No. 1 to the Venture section will not result in a hiatus. This will take much of the weight for training from your shoulders and lay it where it will perform a useful function. Make sure that such skilled groups do not develop into cliques. They must be called upon to share their skill and knowledge, and should contribute to the whole project by comparing methods with others.

Such a core activity might need to be a 'neutral' one which would give scope to many interests. Preparing a local guide book might provide such a long term interest for all, but generally speaking it would be better to engage in something more physical and something which is more exclusively 'Scout-like.' An example, forestry, is detailed here but reference to the Scout Progress Scheme will provide many more themes.

FORESTRY

With transport any Troop should be able to get to the country once a month (even during a week-night). Explore the possibility of developing a small plantation. Very often a farmer has a corner or an unploughable section which has become overgrown. Approach carefully and offer to clear the area and plant trees suitable for fence posts. If you appear trustworthy and are unlikely to be a nuisance he might agree. Then contact your parents to see if you can get the promise of cars for the first Friday or Saturday of every month. Now plan your programme.

Don't thrash into the area cutting down all you see (in fact, you will not be allowed by the Forestry Act to cut more than 125 cubic feet of timber unless the trees are dangerous or diseased). Spend some time in surveying the area, and armed with details of aspect, drainage, vegetation and soil samples seek advice from such Organisations as Men of the Trees, Royal Forestry Society, Society of Foresters or the Forestry Commission.

You might need equipment additional to the Troop axes and bushman's saw. For instance, if you have to deal with mature timber you will need cross-cut, wedges, sledge-hammer, chain saw and, possibly, a high pruner. If a large area has to be cleared, don't plant up too much or you will find little time left for other aspects of Scouting. Half-an-acre could hold a mixed bag of about a thousand young trees (say oak, ash, Scots pine, spruce and larch). One or two square chain might be a more suitable target at first. Try to organise the work so that individual boys can be responsible for all operations concerned with a particular group of trees.

Arrange for someone to demonstrate the techniques of preparing the ground, planting, brashing (cutting lower branches) and thinning. After the trees are planted they must be kept free of vegetation for 3 or 4 years by cutting it away with a hook. This is done in late June or July. Plan your thinning over at least ten years to make the best use of the timber. At an early stage you might make good profits from the sale of Norway Spruce for Christmas trees. Later, ash staves and walking sticks and evergreens for posts and rails will maintain interest. Don't expect quick results, but above all beware the excitement of felling a mature tree: it takes a long time to replace. Do see that any felled tree is properly logged and the brash burned. Nothing will alienate your farmer host quicker than to find his machinery chewing up wood chips or having to extract a stump left several feet above ground level.

Even if you are unable to maintain this interest by producing a Troop of foresters you will at least have the satisfaction of developing a positive rather than a destructive approach to trees. You should see less of the bark carving and axe swinging to lop leading shoots which unfortunately often accompanies the early stages of our axemanship.

If you don't want to get as deeply involved as this, offer your services to a larger conservation group. Surrey Scouts have a County Adviser for Conservation. If your County is not yet Conservation minded, contact the National Trust, Council for Nature or your County Naturalists Trust to see what use they can make of a group of willing horses. You should certainly make the effort to see something of our woodland close to, for now tree recognition has disappeared from the Progress Scheme there is a danger that the use of the axe will dominate. A few hours will be well employed provided observation is detailed and not aimless. In order to do this, the following method is suggested:

STUDY OF A WOOD

Choose some representative sample areas in your stretch of woodland. Mark out ten-yard squares with sisal and pegs. Fill in on a scale drawing (1″ = 1 yard) the location of all trees and name them. Then, with the help of further sisal lengths making a one-yard grid, locate all bushes, shrubs, plants, mosses, fungi, signs of wild life, etc. Take temperature and soil tests and mark position. If you have a camera light meter, take various readings from ground level to the main source of light. Examine the soil. Is it dry or damp; is it bare or covered; what sort of soil is it? Note the date, time and the weather conditions during your visit. Make a neat display copy of your plan and add any specimens gathered.

You may employ this technique in other types of country. It is one sure way of getting boys to use their eyes and appreciate the richness of a natural habitat.

Having covered the range of activities from short wide games to activities lasting for years, don't forget sport. There is a tremendous demand for this from the younger element, which tends to be ignored because a Troop is thought to be too small a unit to find a team. Certainly, a Troop of 30 is not likely to produce a football team able to compete with a school of 300, but there is no reason why other Troops in the district shouldn't be challenged. Better still, choose an activity like fencing, tennis or judo, which requires fewer competitors. This sort of activity calls for a coach or team manager other than the Scout Leader: the Venture Section is most likely to be able to supply such an enthusiast.

The activity chosen need not be physically stretching. Most boys like fishing, but they rarely get an opportunity of plumbing the depths of this pursuit. Two or three at a time might be taken on by local angling club members. Try to cover the range of waters as well as the types of fishing (you might be able to include shark fishing at summer camp!) Archaeology, astronomy, bird watching, all come within this category and somewhere in your neighbourhood is an enthusiast longing to indoctrinate others.

Now, what must you consider in putting an activity before your Scouts?

PRE-PLANNING

Having chosen the activity, decide what type of group will be involved. Generally, this will be a Patrol, but certain activities such as fishing might need special arrangements, or appeal is such that only the older boy takes part. Don't be too concerned to see your Patrols broken apart for certain activities, but do see that they are together for long-term major activities. Give the older Scout a chance to enjoy the company of his contemporaries only on some occasions. This will also give the eleven-year-old the time to move at his own rate so that he isn't pushed too fast in physically stretching activities. Don't under-estimate the potential of the younger group but beware of the danger of setting too great a pace so that they become over-confident.

Next you should consider the parts of the Progress Scheme a Scout will want to pass. Don't let badge regulations dominate your programme or you will find too rigid a pattern emerging. Make the activity interesting first and then devise ways of incorporating the tests or you may lose most of the joy.

ORGANISATION

You will need to cover the ground yourself beforehand and then you should consider what help you will need. This might mean contacting a specialist Organisation to seek for instruction, or joining the Youth Hostels Association or the Ramblers' Association for the use of accommodation facilities. If you are unable to do this yourself the District Activities Adviser should be enlisted to help. If it is a case of training the whole Troop, the Local Education Authority may be prepared to arrange a course if you can promise attendance from 15 members, though most likely you will find the lower age limit will be 14 years old.

Transport might be a major factor and if your own parents and supporters cannot help, the District Activities Adviser might try to arrange a sharing with other Troops.

Equipment will be needed if you are engaging on an activity new to the Troop. Seek help; you cannot afford to make a poor choice with the limited funds at your disposal. Try to buy your own gear if the project is to last for some time. Otherwise, you might have to borrow from the Local Education Authority or the District store. Some Local Education Authorities are prepared to make grants or loans towards new equipment but the approach must be made through the District Commissioner.

Don't take on all the work yourself. Delegate equipment, transport, route finding and feeding to the Patrol Leaders.

DRESS

P.O.R. suggests that you dress appropriately for the activity. This means that you should be prepared for difficult conditions, but don't let the flexibility of our regulations be an excuse for sloppiness. See that your Scouts are smart and appear well equipped when in public. Don't let arguments about warmth mean balaclavas in the High Street. (See chapter on Troop Administration.)

YOUR PART

There is a tendency to believe that you have to lead all activities, that you possess all the qualities you are trying to encourage in your boys. Personal leadership is important for the younger element but once boys reach an age where they want to develop in their own interests they cease to be a unified group to some extent. You cannot lead them at all times then. Your job will be to provide general direction and to entrust others to supply certain skills. To be a good director you need to be able to make the best use of other people's skills: the skills of your boys and the skills of experts from elsewhere. You also need to know your own limitations, and the limitations of your experts and those of your boys. Try to work only from their strength so that you are operating on the level at which each is most capable.

It will be your task also to provide the right 'tone' for your

Troop's activity. Some Leaders will produce a 'hearty' Troop, others might be concerned with values on a much deeper level. You might tend to overstress the function of an activity and make something like country dancing dominate the life of the Troop. Remember that you are a Scouter; remember, too, that the Law and the Promise lie at the back of all the training of a good Scout. By all means engage in country dancing as your sole pursuit but see that you permeate it with the true ethos of Scouting. As long as you are doing well, better than others might, and fully use the Scout method, you might not be doing the Movement a dis-service.

FOLLOW UP

To make full use of the values of your chosen activity you will need to exchange ideas with others, perhaps compete with them, and use a specialised vocabulary to make your ideas more precise. To further these purposes it would be worth joining the Society concerned with encouraging the activity. At the very least you should subscribe to the magazine serving this activity. Consult your Public Library about the choice but aim to have your own copy for reference and to stimulate the interest of your boys.

SUMMER CAMP

Thoughts of the annual camp have been left to the end of this chapter because this should be a natural culmination to your planning for the year. This means that the training provided by your activities, preferably your major activity, can be put to the test. The skills learnt over odd hours during the week or at week-ends can now be integrated and fully related over a period of one or two weeks. Archaeologists will be able to see some results, foresters will be able to scale up their interest, explorers of the local canal will be able to cruise a whole canal system, collectors of local lore or folk dancers might enjoy exchanging enthusiasms with those on the Continent. Most important, a boy will be able to live and talk his interest without pause and to his fill.

Obviously such a specialised annual camp will not appeal to all. If you are operating from a base camp you will be able to meet the needs of the newer recruits in providing the traditional camp programme.

Others might enjoy providing for their specialist contemporaries through quartermastering. Generally, you will find all will enjoy the opportunity of doing something positive rather than merely living under canvas. With Instructor help you might be able to mount several specialist pursuits from the same base camp. A camp in the Pyrenees would thrill all Scouts, provide scope for geologists, speleologists and mountaineers, enliven a study of local customs or transhumance, or provide a comparison with a survey of an English village. Add music, mapping, photography or what you will and few would opt out of such an experience.

Chapter 13

ADVENTURE ACTIVITIES

Within the narrow confines of one chapter it is impossible to give an adequate guide to all adventure activities. There is already a tremendous amount of experience within the Movement regarding air and water activities. You can do no better than make use of the appropriate Headquarters departments for Air and Sea Activities if you wish to pursue any of these activities (but there are chapters in this Handbook which will give you some guidance on such matters). In this chapter you will find suggested lines of development for a few activities only, but the more detailed scheme for climbing should give you an indication of the type of planning needed for all adventure activities. Any adventurous pursuit should be treated in much the same way as the major activities discussed in the previous chapter, so refer back to the end of that chapter for the methods of planning.

The main difference between adventure activities and those previously discussed is the degree of hazard involved, so a number of safeguards should be considered before you commit yourself to action. Firstly, it is most important to get proper guidance. You will be able to provide some direction, but you are unlikely to have the judgement or the skill to make a leader in more than one of the pursuits in which boys would like to engage. Do get help, but see that your helper is properly trained. There are many people who claim a knowledge of an adventurous activity but before accepting them at face value see that they have the training and experience to hold the lives of your boys in their hands. Your Activities Adviser or Headquarters will advise on minimum requirements, or be able to put you in touch with Organisations and Clubs devoted to the activity in which you are interested.

Then consider that there might be occasions when the boys will find conditions such that they will be in difficulty. To meet such an emergency they must be trained to react effectively. A knowledge of the safety requirements for the activity is essential, but it must be more than a knowledge of theory. There should be a built-in automatic response which will only come with practice and not from a reading of the safety rules. Consider first the safety rules which follow but then see that there are many opportunities for what can be called 'survival training.'

SAFETY RULES

Every adventure activity has its own set of safety rules. These will be taught by your specialist instructor and it is your responsibility to see that all the rules are understood and practised by the boys at all times. Know how and where to get help. It is important to see that you are up to date and that you have all the relevant literature for the activity you are pursuing. (The Sports Council and the Royal Society for the Prevention of Accidents produce booklets which should be available in sufficient quantity for instructors as well as for Patrols.)

Clothing

Wear appropriate garments and have a reserve available for unplanned conditions. For most outdoor activities the boys will need woollen underclothing, long-sleeved shirt, woollen socks, long-sleeved jersey and thick trousers (because of their poor insulation value in cold or wet conditions, jeans should never be worn). Individual adventure activities will require additional clothing and equipment, e.g. boiler suits and helmets for caving, ropes and waterproof outers for climbing, life-jackets for boating.

Food

Always carry a reserve supply of food such as chocolate,

glucose sweets and dried fruit, which you must resist the temptation to nibble.

Precautions

Leave word of your destination and don't change your plans without correcting these instructions. Keep your party together and have someone responsible bringing up the rear. Give yourself plenty of time, plus a margin for accidents. If at any height do not throw or dislodge stones. Be as watchful once your objective is achieved; this is particularly important when descending a mountain, for most accidents seem to occur then. Be familiar with distress procedure (six long flashes/notes in *quick* succession repeated at one-minute intervals, or the S.O.S. morse signal . . . — — — . . .). Make sure you read and own a copy of *Safety on the Hills* (2nd Edition) which can be obtained from the Scout Shop for 5p.

When boating, be able to swim fifty yards fully clothed; don't wear knee boots. See that the appropriate permission or Charge Certificate is held.

This cannot be a comprehensive guide to safety precautions. See that the detail is covered by your Instructor and the boys understand the reasons by reading an authoritative textbook.

Check for each particular activity regularly, for as each becomes more sophisticated so you will find that the safety requirements need to be modified.

Survival Training

The basic training must be first-aid. See that the Troop is familiar with treatment for exposure, shock, rope burns, drowning as well as for fractures, sprains, wounds, and cramp. Very high on the list of priorities also should come swimming. There has been such intensive effort at primary school level that very often this may be restricted to testing (A.S.A. survival awards) or training in 'drownproofing' techniques (see *Drownproofing* by F. Lanoue, at your local library). This latter skill is concerned with staying afloat in deep water until help arrives. It is particularly valuable for weak swimmers or for countering cramp, which is a hazard for the strongest swimmers. Making make-shift buoyancy aids from trousers, shirts, upturned bucket or even gumboots should be practised, although it should be stressed that these are no substitute for life-jackets for deep-water sailors. During the winter months Troop Meetings might start a little later to enable a swimming session, taken by the baths instructor, to be run first.

Short sessions of 'backwoods' Scouting might find their place in the survival programme. Making bivouacs, smoke signals, heliograph signals, direction finding without compass, fire without matches, would all make more sense to the average boy if seen as part of survival training. Take it seriously and see that an integrated programme (which includes talks on insulation and exposure, etc.) is prepared, rather than filling the odd gaps in the meeting with gimmick quickies.

CLIMBING

Assuming that the pre-planning stages mentioned in the previous chapter have been covered, an introduction to one adventure activity might be time-tabled in the following manner.

First, obtain the services of an Instructor: someone who knows his subject, has the necessary equipment to arouse interest, and who can call on the services of climbing companions when leaders are needed. It cannot be over-emphasized that the Instructor should be fully qualified and preferably the holder of the Mountain Leadership Certificate.

Week 1

Introduce your Instructor to the Troop during an indoor meeting. He might make use of film or slides to stimulate interest, but as far as possible encourage the boys to get the feel of the equipment — rope, sling, karabiners, boots. Suggest that he might glamourise the activity by abseiling out of the window, by prussicking out of a 'crevasse' or by showing the danger of running nylon over nylon. This should not be the only item in the programme; it is mainly to sell the activity to the Troop, though you should have won the Patrol Leaders over already for it to be in the programme. Have some literature on climbing available so that they can read about it at home. This will keep interest alive until the next meeting and will establish a good atmosphere more quickly. This literature should always be available, not because theory is so important but because a special vocabulary is an important means of communication in most adventure activities and only by assimilating it can a novice feel in tune with a group of enthusiasts. After this meeting you might arrange for the older boys to join a Local Education Authority or C.C.P.R. course, though in some cases it would be better if this came later.

Week 2

This will take up almost the whole meeting time; so, if you haven't aroused the interest of all, it might need to be arranged on another evening or at the week-end.

Introduction to climbing knots, ropework and belaying technique; handling 120-foot ropes; climbing sequence in threes, using recognised 'calls.' All this can be done indoors, using beams or radiators, or outdoors from a tree, and all at ground level. Then the group should split up and get the feel of holds only a few feet from the ground. After demonstration, they should work at hand jams, finger-holds, lay-backs, mantelshelf, and generally appreciate the balance and movement involved. A good instructor should be able to improvise enough holds to occupy a group in most types of building. The climbing will be done on this occasion in plimsolls, though if suitable rough stone walling is available they would be better employed getting the feel of their boots. The Instructor should have enough ropes available for this evening (probably discarded climbing ropes), but from now on you must have access to enough rope for all your group. (District store?)

Week 3

Travel to the nearest outcrop or quarry for the day. One Instructor can supervise three ropes of three climbers if everyone is top-roped from above, though it is desirable for the correction of early faults to have an Instructor for each rope. Start with the holds covered last week, then straight easy routes (no traversing), some practice in holding short falls, abseiling. Keep your eyes open for the natural leaders and the 'tigers.' A good instructor will be able to pack six hours full of interest. Return to Headquarters (or, better still, a climbing club hut if you are lucky) and plan next week's expedition over coffee. Let the boys suggest the clothing, equipment, transport and food so that they feel it is their show. If there are other climbers about, you will soon find the right spirit of camaraderie developing.

Week 4

Camp at an outcrop which has found its way into a guide book. Let the boys read of the climbs and explain the technical jargon to them. Plan to cook for the morning and evening only and carry a packet meal to the face (remember that meat sandwiches tend to be indigestible; better to nibble chocolate, cheese, sweets and fruit at intervals). Limit the week-end to those who have covered all previous training and expect some camping experience as well. Some non-climbers may accompany the party to run the base camp; this might be a good opportunity for you to train new recruits if no Patrol Leader is available.

Continue top-roped climbing on some of the more difficult routes, but include some routes led by the Instructor to put some spice into the week-end. Encourage your party to mix with other experienced climbers. This is a good opportunity to learn the vocabulary of climbing and develop an eye for route-finding.

Week 5

A repetition of Week 4 would be valuable. Have an indoor meeting to prepare for the first mountain trip. Clothing and equipment should be checked; map and compass work revised; discuss mountain walking and safety. Show pictures and guide books of the area to be visited.

Week 6

Plan a week-end in Snowdonia, the Lakes, the Peaks or Scotland. Stay at a Youth Hostel or, if you are lucky, your Instructor might be able to arrange to take the party as his guests to a club hut. Insist on the proper courtesy to other hostellers and sit on the tendency to act tough: your lads might think they know the ropes at this stage.

Spend one whole day on a high ridge scramble in spite of objections from the boys. Use the time fully to ensure plenty of practice with map and compass, discussion about routes down as well as up, safety (the sudden dropping of mist or darkness and where to lie up.) Demonstrate the importance of this training if ever they are to go off without an Instructor. They should learn the value of boots to provide support to the ankles, and the treachery of steep grass. Encourage conversation with the 'regulars,' once you have warned your party to be modest.

Travelling home will cut into the second day considerably. Spend the morning on a long abseil (with safety rope) to give the boys a sense of exposure, and top-roped boulder climbing to get the feel of the local rock. This exercise is important if all the climbing to date has been on low sandstone outcrops.

Week 7

Week-end to Snowdonia, the Lakes or Scotland (staying at a Youth Hostel or camping). Main feature of the week-end to be a couple of 'moderate' or easy 'difficult' climbs on one of the well-known nursery crags, e.g. Milestone Buttress on Tryfan. On this rock climbing week-end one Instructor should lead not more than two boys on a rope.

At this stage you will be able to assess the amount of time to give to this activity in future and what form it will take. Do they show more enthusiasm for rock climbing or for the long scrambles in the mountains? Will you be spending regular short sessions on a near-by outcrop or saving up for the longer expedition among our own mountains, or perhaps travelling abroad to the Pyrenees and the Alps? If the enthusiasm is there, you must start providing your own equipment, making more formal contact with a club and setting up your own internal organisation for furthering the activity.

If enthusiasm is not general, you must see that the odd Scout who has been bitten is provided for. Arrange for him to go on recognised courses (through your Activities Adviser or H.Q.) and see that he joins other like-minded brethren in another Troop (or later, a Venture Unit keen on climbing). Discourage the enthusiast from going it alone even if you have to pay for his membership to a recognised club. Even if you are sure that the Troop has had enough, don't drop the activity like a hot brick with "now we've done climbing, what next?" Don't waste the skills and equipment you have acquired but utilise them in a new direction. For instance, why not orienteering? This is a sport with a dedicated following which involves crossing difficult country on a series of precise compass bearings. Whereas your compass has been an ancillary aid, now you will have to rely entirely on your skill to use it to within an accuracy of a hundred yards or less. You will certainly develop a better eye for the country and a more satisfying thrill from the interpretation of contours. The competitive element will stimulate your interest and provide as sharp an edge as the exposure of a lofty climb.

CAVING

The training programme for this activity might be organised on the same pattern as that for climbing though it might prove more difficult to find reliable Instructors. A visit to a show cave or a mine could be arranged as an introduction, for there is no way of simulating the feeling of claustrophobia which some may feel underground.

The first pieces of equipment obtained should be a miner's helmet or fibre helmet (British Standards Specification 2826) and reliable lighting — carbide or electric. A boiler suit is likely to prove the most useful outer garment you can wear, although any old but strong clothes will do. Because of the more regular contact with damp, see that most of the clothing is made of wool. Old Army boots are preferable to expensive climbing boots. Avoid lacing hooks and tricouni nails, which can be a danger on wire ladders.

To climbing techniques (see Week 2, Climbing) add the use of wire ladders during your Headquarters' training, but as soon as possible get below ground. In known caves with only one route it will be possible to use boy leaders at an earlier stage than for climbing, but always see that safety precautions are observed to the letter (spare food, clothing and lighting as well as informing an 'outsider' of your destination).

When exploring a new system see that you make full use of local knowledge even if your Instructor is an acknowledged expert. Include exercises in mapping, rescue from a restricted space, route finding, coping with sumps, and, later, making rubberised suits for wet caves. Even at an early stage take in some wet caves and ones with short ladder pitches so that progression is positive. During the evenings don't fight shy of technical talks by experts on limestone topography and geology underground, photography and minerology. A knowledge of the time scale involved would be most effective in preventing damage to formations and other thoughtless acts below ground.

A great deal of interest and fun will be obtained from the most elementary caves, for the scale and difficulty cannot be assessed by the beginner so easily as during climbing sessions. But to follow the full development of this sport more stamina is needed than in rock climbing. It will require climbing skill, but it also demands the fitness to wriggle for hours, possibly while soaking wet. Don't go too far with youngsters; they will be absolutely thrilled with the most rudimentary work-outs.

The best areas for caving are Glamorgan, Pembroke, the Mendips, Devon, the Peak District and the Yorkshire Dales.

RIDING

Riding is an experience which is well worth including among the 'musts' for our activity list. We all fancy ourselves astride a horse, but when an opportunity comes we are frightened off by the size of the animal. The first hour in the saddle is more like the struggle of wills between St. George and the dragon, little of the image of man and his faithful mount. Thus we see the value of the time spent in the stables, grooming and ordering the tangle of leather which makes up the bridle. Before springing into the saddle you must establish a relationship. Becoming part of the unit 'horse and rider' is often a more revealing experience than matching yourself against the elements. This is why it is such a worthwhile activity for all Scouts.

Pony clubs and riding courses abound. It might be possible for a stable to arrange a short introductory course for every Scout. Even this might be enough, but try to follow with a Summer Camp pony trekking. For equipment you will need little more than strong trousers and a pair of gloves. It will be hard work but an experience you will treasure.

CANOEING

Few people are too far from sea, river, canal or lake to take some interest in water activities. To establish an interest the most useful craft is the canoe, because it is cheap and can be used in under six inches of water. Much can be done without regular Instructors in attendance, though like all sports proper training will produce a deeper satisfaction.

If you have the space it is an excellent winter activity to build your own canoes. Choose the plans only after consultation. Single-seaters of good design will allow for more advanced techniques and more room for kit. There is sufficient help and know-how available within the Movement (Percy Blandford) to omit details here. But, before you start, consider storage of the finished canoes. Most boys will be able to keep their own canoe at home, though you might wish to make this a Troop project, at your expense, so that the canoes can be kept together and under more positive supervision. Make sure that they are easily accessible and not wedged so securely in the rafters of Headquarters that they just gather dust. Then you will need transport to get them to the water. If this is to be a Troop activity it would be worth considering a proper trailer so that you can all move together.

Once the canoes are built, plan a training programme to ensure that you get maximum benefit from your new form of transport. Many Local Education Authorities offer training courses; if yours doesn't, you can be put in touch with the nearest club. At the same time see that everyone can swim. Aim to achieve a minimum standard of fifty yards clothed, but expect the canoe captains to be able to life-save and swim something like two hundred yards in clothes. A marked improvement in swimming standards should be one of the side effects of taking up water activities.

After a few sessions covering balance, trim, paddling and capsizing, you should be able to supervise most inland activities yourself. See that you follow our boating regulations to the letter though. You will obviously start by paddling about on your nearest stretch of water, however limited, but as soon as possible plan to do a journey by canal or river. For a start the canal is the most likely choice, but warn the boys of the portaging involved to get around locks.

From the beginning train your canoeists to take quick evasive action to avoid obstructions (weirs, tree trunks, stakes, wire, etc.). Check on the ownership of the water and see that you don't upset fishermen by paddling through their lines.

After a journey involving an over-night stop, you can register your needs in regard to your canoe. Only after twenty-four hours will you have the experience to judge the value of spray covers, drip rings, long painters, buoyancy bags, back rests, waterproof kitbags, sponges for bailing, repair kit and even a trolley. This journey will tell you something of the other problems, such as the difficulty in finding shops close to the water (you might need a cycling outrider for somewhere like the Oxford Canal) and the need to carry drinking water. Spend the next week-end working (and discussing) together to correct the faults you have found. Then start planning a more ambitious journey. There are a number of worthwhile canoeing rivers, but check the waters first. The best way would be to have some of the Troop join an organised cruise and then let them lead your group on the same journey. Stanfords produce a map of the canoeing waters of the British Isles which will save you a deal of leg work.

You need not limit your canoeing to smooth water cruising. Tidal estuaries call for some seamanship involving a knowledge of tides, winds and the rule of the 'road,' so you would need to put your training in the hands of a recognised expert. Similarly, you will need help if you plan to engage in white water canoeing, competitive racing, slalom or sailing with lee-boards. Whatever the development don't let the programme become static. Plan ahead. It is very easy for messing about in canoes on the nearest lake to kill any real interest the boys might have. Plan the full extension of your activity from the start. If only one boy has the enthusiasm to progress to white water canoeing, you should see that you make arrangements for him to do so with a reputable body. There is sufficient skill and lore in this activity to keep the interest of the Troop all the while. See that they have the opportunity to drink their fill. Arrange affiliated membership of the British Canoe Union, make contact with your nearest club and subscribe to a magazine which will keep you in touch with latest developments.

If canoeing is too 'shallow' an interest for your lads, you might enlarge to the wider complex of boating activities. If you found that canoe building was the source of their enthusiasm, why not plan to build a sailing dinghy (or something bigger) or, if your waters are restricted, perhaps you might get more fun from raft building. If little ability in construction or skill in water craft was apparent, turn their attention to our seafaring tradition — lighthouses, lifeboats and the merchant marine — or trace the development of our canal system through a series of hikes and visits.

Start with the facilities you can find at hand and explore the possibilities of extending the interest further. Don't be put off by a few difficulties.

To some extent the depth of the boys' interest and the range of their exploration will depend on your ability. If you are no carpenter it is likely that you will be too timid to awaken any enthusiasm for boat building. Realise this, and realise also that it is your duty as a Leader to provide, through others, the capabilities which you yourself lack. We have in Sea Scouting, Instructors and a training medium second to none. Make use of this experience and skill; though you will find all boatmen very ready to give a helping hand. Make use of the courses and the craft available within the Movement. There is no reason at all why you shouldn't sail to your Summer Camp (even if it is on the Continent) if you can find an experienced skipper in need of a crew.

The sea calls most of us on this island and there is something of the heritage of a thousand years of seafaring waiting to be tapped in all Scouts. You will get plenty of ideas from our Sea Activities literature, just as you will find the twentieth century medium — the air — well covered by Air Activities. Remember that all these activities — gliding, parascending, sailing, etc. — are as much your oyster as they are for the specialist Sea and Air Troops.

Finally, and in special relation to this chapter and the previous one, we would add that most specialist Organisations and Bodies possess their own headquarters. These Organisations are invariably ready and willing to provide advice and help and, if their addresses are not readily available, enquiries to the Programme and Training Department at Headquarters will in most cases result in your obtaining the information you require.

Chapter 14

SPECIAL EVENTS

Just as in our everyday lives we look forward to anniversaries and red letter days, so all worthwhile Troops have shown that a few special events during the year enrich the Troop's life. How many and of what nature will inevitably vary according to the circumstances of the Troop. The suggested events which follow can be found in the programmes of many Troops and some of them, at least, could be adopted by all. Although a number of these events, indeed most of them, will concern the Group as a whole, nevertheless the Troop will play a large part both previous to and during the occasion.

Four general points should be made:

(i) Thorough and detailed preparation is necessary, whatever the event: the "it will be all right on the night" mentality courts disaster.

(ii) Common sense should be used when choosing date, time and place for your occasion. (For example, the Troop which holds a garden party on the afternoon of the Cup Final deserves to have a flop on its hands! We recall a National Scout Conference which wasn't allowed to start until the broadcast of a certain International Rugger match had ended!) In the same way, the availability of buses (or trains) must be considered if people are expected from some way afield: in the suburbs of big cities and towns fathers must be given time to reach home and have their meals, etc.

(iii) The programme at your first event will largely influence the attendance at your second! In other words, make the programme enjoyable and worthwhile for those attending.
(iv) Whatever the occasion, the dates should be settled and invitations sent out well in advance. Indeed, a well-organised Group will plan its year many months ahead.

PARENTS' AND SONS' SCOUTS' OWN SERVICES

Whether a Troop holds regular Scouts' Own Services or not, one annual service which parents and friends can attend is highly desirable. Two times of the year stand out as being more suitable than others: February 22nd, B.-P.'s birthday, and just before Christmas, when even parents who are not regular churchgoers like to join in some familiar carols and take part in a Christmas Service.

As in every event, the Patrol Leaders' Council should, in conjunction with the Leaders (and of course with the Troop Chaplain if there is one) consider the details of the service. The keynotes should be simplicity and — within reason — brevity; the patterns can be various but hearty singing of well-known hymns, suitable prayers which might be led by a Patrol Leader (*Scout Prayers* published by The Scout Association is an essential for every Troop), a lesson (or lessons) read by carefully rehearsed Scouts, who should be encouraged particularly to hold up their heads and speak out the words boldly to the congregation and not mumble them, and a *brief* address.

B.-P.'s words on the subject should be remembered: "Short hymns (three verses are as a rule quite enough — never more than four); understandable prayers; a good address from a man who really understands boys" — and, one might add here, parents too! B.-P. continues: "If a man cannot make his point to keen boys in ten minutes he ought to be shot." An accomplished pianist is a great help but no musical accompaniment is better than a poor one. Scouts who play guitars well might easily practise the hymn tunes and lay down a fine beat for the singing.

CHRISTMAS PARTY

This should be a dignified affair when good manners prevail and everyone within the bounds of happiness is on his — and her — good behaviour. For this is essentially an occasion when the invitations — and it is an excellent thing for proper invitation cards to be used — are for each Scout and a girl friend, and in that definition sisters may be permitted! So the boys and girls arrive in their best leisure clothes and the programme must be equal to such appearance: this is *NOT* an evening for British Bulldogs! The following points may be helpful:

(1) The party should be free: i.e. any expenses incurred should come from Troop/Group funds.

(2) Mothers of Scouts should be asked some time beforehand to be prepared to provide the wherewithal for the meal — cakes, tinned fruit, filling for sandwiches, jellies, sausage rolls, tea, sugar, etc.

(3) A Christmas Tree with a gift for everyone may be beyond some Troops, but helps the spirit of the occasion as well as looking well, lit up and loaded!

(4) The boys themselves and fathers as well as Venture Scouts can all co-operate to make themselves responsible for the decorations: a Committee of mothers should be invited to prepare the food and drink.

(5) The Patrol Leaders' Council should be consulted as to the details of the entertainment — remembering that young people are much more sophisticated than they used to be and may prefer more dancing than games: although some of each is probably the answer. Small prizes are always appreciated.

(6) Five-thirty till nine-thirty (or six till ten) is probably the best time, but some of the eleven and twelve-year-olds may have to leave early. A good meal and then plenty of soft drink, and tea and coffee should be available during the evening.

(7) Someone, "a host," should be on duty to welcome the guests — perhaps the Scout Leader — and also to say 'good night' and give the young people an opportunity of saying 'thank you.'

THE ANNUAL SHOW

This is surely the oldest of Scout red letter occasions, for there are at least a few Troops who have a record of fifty or so consecutive shows. Nevertheless it should not be entered upon lightly. For whereas there is no more potentially valuable and worthwhile occasion — in helping the Scouts to grow in confidence, and to develop their talents, and none is recollected in later life with more affection ("These are the days we shall dream about and we'll call them the good old days") — yet the preparation and rehearsing of a show involves long hours of planning and much anxiety.

On the other hand the pleasure a good Troop or Group Show can give, not only to the triumphant performers but to the audiences (with golden opinions gained for Scouting not only for the proud parents but for the community in which the Troop exists) is more than reward for the days of doubt and endeavour.

It would need (it *does* need!) a book to deal adequately with the Troop Show, but the following brief notes will be of some assistance:

1. The business side and the producer's side should be kept entirely separate.

2. In considering the date for the show, the availability of the Scouts is all important. Many Troops find the Easter school holiday or the week's holiday now customary at half-term to be the best performance days for the good of the boys for obvious reasons.

3. A timetable of rehearsals should be planned in advance so that the performers and others concerned (pianist, stage manager, props assistant, lighting assistant, etc.) can be aware of their commitments. It is also vitally important that parents are kept fully informed of what is expected of their sons.

4. The *type* of show must be decided upon, depending on the presumed talent available in the Troop, the amount of past experience, and the size of the stage or other acting area. One can divide Scout shows into three categories: (i) the two- or three-act play with or without music (Ralph Reader has written several excellent examples of these for Scouts); (ii) the show of two or three one-act plays; (iii) the revue or variety type of entertainment of the "Gang Show" kind. The last is probably most within the compass of Troops doing a show for the first time.

5. The Business Manager (a layman if possible) sees to the budgeting and finance, to the printing and sale of tickets and posters; the reserving of the hall and the provision of

extra chairs if necessary; any advertisement thought advisable; to having the programmes printed and to obtaining any advertisements from local well-wishers to help with the cost; the provision of stewards and programme sellers for the actual performances — and, in fact, everything to do with the event not concerned directly with the actual show or the performers. Press relations are very important too.

6. If a Troop is producing an original play or sketch it must be licensed by the Lord Chamberlain before it can be performed (Address: St. James's Palace, London, S.W.1). A fee will be requested.

7. The Stage Manager and the Producer will need assistants to be responsible for scripts and properties, for lighting, for costumes, and a prompter.

8. Rehearsals should start (and end) punctually and be planned so that the Scouts do not feel they're merely hanging about: boys easily get bored. A rehearsal one evening a week for three months will not be found too much.

9. The help of Mums (for costumes) and Dads (for props) can be enlisted.

10. Make-up is all important: help is usually most generously given by experts in local Amateur Dramatic Societies. The Junior Drama League and the Drama League might be asked to assist too.

11. One *good* pianist is sufficient for most Troop shows: two *good* pianists are even better.

12. Advice as to sketches, songs, etc., that are available can be obtained from Headquarters.

All this, it must be appreciated, is in the briefest outline. Until that much-needed book on the subject comes to be written, the best advice perhaps for a beginner is to find an experienced Scouter in your own or a nearby District to advise, encourage (and if necessary) console you!

TROOP PARTY FOR OTHERS

For those, that is, who perhaps don't have too many parties, like many old people who are lonely or poor or both, or like boys whose only home is a Home (and however good, perhaps a little monotonous.)

Old folk first: the details must depend on circumstances,

facilities and funds available. But the old folk should be collected in cars: this can be done by fathers, old Scouts or members of Rotary or Round Table and brought to the Hall, which should be smart and decorated and warm. Someone — it will be either mid-morning if it is a lunch party, or mid-afternoon if it is an early-supper party — will welcome them. Coffee, tea, hot milk (or even something stronger if the tenets of the Group permit) could be waiting. But whatever the form of the party (1) the food should be attractive and well presented, (2) there should be entertainment by the Scouts, (3) there should be time for the boys to chat a little with the old folk, who all too often miss most of all just meeting other people.

The party should not go on too long (old folk tire); the seating should be as comfortable as possible. It is very pleasant if each old person can be given a small parcel (a gift) to take home with them — and here parents will need little encouragement to contribute tea and sugar, some chocolate, and so on. A present, especially if *made* by the Scouts, would give extra pleasure.

As for finding the old folk in the first place, if your church does not know enough, a Welfare Officer on the local Council, or the W.V.S. (especially if they run a 'meals on wheels' service) will advise and help. Of course, the Scouts, in their smartest uniforms, must be there to serve and help in every way possible.

As for the Barnardo or other such boys (Local Authorities may have information about Homes for orphan children which are located in your area), what they want will be fun and a change of atmosphere — and plenty to eat and drink and some games (if possible with inexpensive prizes). One can explain this event best perhaps by saying that, for that particular evening, Troop Night is a party night as well and the guests become honorary members for the evening and, where circumstances permit, it might even be possible to invite some of these boys to become members of the Troop.

In both cases, see — it is worth one more reminder — that invitations are sent well in advance and all the details of time, place and transport are very clear to all.

TROOP BIRTHDAY PARTY

The details must depend on the Troop: not to forget the occasion and so to build up a tradition is the main thing. It can be just a simple evening of games, with a sing-song and some reminiscence ("the time I remember most in my Scouting") or can be an elaborate affair with a brief thanksgiving service, combined with a display of photographs, log books, models, handicrafts, etc., and a sit-down ham and salad supper (mothers are wonderful!) and a toast or two and a ceremonial cutting of the Birthday cake. For it is the birthday cake, appropriately iced and decorated in Troop colours that makes this evening memorable: again, parents are usually extremely generous and skilful, *given a specific object*. When the cake is cut, some should be set aside to be sent to sick members of the Troop, to particular friends or benefactors of the Troop (and perhaps to boys who have left during the year, with a card saying 'from old friends who hope you will be along again one day perhaps'). Of course, the Birthday Party could well be something quite different — a visit to a show, dining out, etc. The great thing is to observe the occasion.

INVESTITURE NIGHT

The ceremony for an Investiture can be as simple as a Troop's traditions allow. For the Scout to be invested surely this particular evening ranks as the most important in his life as a Scout. It is suggested elsewhere in this book that the parents of the Scout concerned should be invited to be present. Parents *ARE* a part of Scouting.

TROOP OPEN NIGHT

Perhaps once a year parents should be invited to attend a Troop Night, just to see what goes on. The minimum of alteration of the normal programme should take place. Only two changes are recommended:

(1) Before each game or project or instruction the Scouter should explain what is going to happen, particularly (with games) the purpose in mind.

(2) For one item a few fathers might be asked to compete against their sons, but not with anything too serious — certainly not first-aid, for example, which should never be

trifled with. The important thing is to recognise the difference between the A.G.M. (where the parents are an integral part of the proceedings and are consciously to be informed and entertained) and an 'Open Night' where they are interested spectators, but where the Scouts' interests must come first, the parents' second.

ANNUAL GENERAL MEETING

A Group affair — in a sense a combined Group Scouters' Meeting and Group Council affair — but a most important occasion in which Scouts from the Troop will play a part. The following points seem generally relevant:

1. Proper invitations, giving time, place, detail of any special entertainment, should be sent well in advance to both parents of a Scout with a footnote "it is hoped that one parent at least will be able to attend and so encourage both their son and his Leaders."

2. The programme can be usefully divided into halves: (a) strictly business reports, (b) refreshments and entertainment.

3. The business programme would follow these lines: (a) welcome to those present by the District Commissioner or the Group Scout Leader or the Chairman of the Group Council, (b) report of the Group Council Secretary on meetings during the year and the part played by them, (c) report of the Group Treasurer, (d) welcoming and introducing new Group Council members while thanking those retiring, (e) brief comments by Scouters on report of the year's events, previously cyclostyled and circulated to parents, (f) proposals for the coming year. All speeches should be brief and factual.

4. Coffee and biscuits, etc., prepared by a Sub-Committee of mothers and served by Patrol Leaders and others (Venture Scouts) should be followed by the entertainment, for example, a demonstration by Cub Scouts and Scouts — or a Scout film.

5. End with a quiet prayer.

6. A hollow square is the best arrangement with rows of chairs on three sides, the speakers on the fourth and the centre of the space for demonstrations.

CAMP REPORT EVENING

Not to report in some way on the Summer Camp is discourteous to parents, whose sons (and money!) have made the camp possible. Some Troops content themselves with a report in a Troop Magazine or Newsletter, but gatherings for Scouts and their parents are a splendid opportunity for propaganda, for increasing confidence and understanding between Scouters and parents, for helping the parents to realise that they are, in the widest sense, a part of the Scout family and, if nothing more, for parents and Scouters to meet.

Camp photographs, etc., could be displayed, and if sound (tape recording) and sight (film or slides) are available, these should be shown.

These should be preceded by a brief report (reviewing weather, programme, menus, costs, etc.) on the camp by the Scouter who had been in charge and "Minilectures" by each Patrol Leader — anecdotal, each dealing perhaps with a particular event, and given in each boy's natural way. The latter, however, should be to the point and, if possible, rehearsed beforehand. The Scouter comes on again at the epilogue, giving details of the Patrol Leaders' Council's hopes (or plans, if sufficiently far ahead) for the next Summer Camp.

SOME OTHER IDEAS:

Guy Fawkes Party. Scouts share their fireworks, have a bonfire, invite some less privileged boys as guests. Mothers offer gingerbread and cocoa at the end, or Scouts cook baked potatoes in the ashes.

Visit to Gilwell (or a H.Q. Camp Site). A coach outing for the day, the site being informed in advance. (Details of camp sites, etc., can be obtained from *The Scout Handbook*).

Visit to the London Gang Show (if you can get tickets!) or to a local or not-too-far-distant Scout Show.

Film Evening. Scout films for boys and parents. Tea and biscuits prepared by Mums or members of the Group Council. (Films can be hired from Sound Services Ltd., Wilton Crescent, London, S.W.19.)

National Events. Does your Troop take part in the National Sea Scout Regatta, National Cooking-in-Camp Competition, Scout Car Races, the National Scout Band Championships, Fathers' and Sons' Camp, International Week-end (the last two normally at Gilwell)? Information can always be had from

Headquarters or Gilwell Park.

Open Day. If you have your own Headquarters, why not mount a display of blown-up camp photos, posters, models, logbooks, etc., and invite any Scouts or interested folk from other Troops along: say from 3 to 6 p.m. one Saturday.

Pancake Cooking Evening. For Shrove Tuesday, by Patrols, over butane gas or other camp cookers. A pancake race could be included. (Patrol prize for best single pancake?)

Cheese and Wine Party. For parents of Scouts, organised by the Group Council (inexpensive tickets, for this is not an event that needs to be paid for from Group funds or provided free by the Group). Object: Scouters and parents, and parents and parents to become better acquainted. Local grocers and wine merchants will advise and often give most generous terms 'for the good of the cause.' Patrol Leaders and Assistant Patrol Leaders to serve. (N.B.—Soft drinks to be provided for *them*!)

All-Night Hike. Can be a memory for a lifetime. Parents should be informed secretly of the route to be taken, but a 'secret' destination is more fun for the Scouts. A series of talks on hiking (care of feet, proper clothes, etc.) should precede the occasion, which is best detailed to begin on Friday evening. Arrangements for a halfway snack (hot soup with bread is best) can be made, either by carrying one's own supplies or by arrangement with another Troop along the route. Breakfast — lavish and hot, as guests of another Troop (for whom later you can return the compliment) or back at one's own Headquarters, cooked by supporters under whatever name or by old Scouts, Venture Scouts, or ever-loving Mums, makes this a wonderful memory for all — even if the weather doesn't turn out to be all that it should! Every Scout should see the dawn rising once!

And one could go on: the Winter Bazaar, the Garden Party — there is at least one Troop where fathers play their Scout sons at football on Boxing Day morning!

The weeks, the months, the years go by: and boyhood is over. Boyhood is the sum of individual hours: at the end the boy, and the man he is soon to become, is the result not only of his heredity and of his environment but of a hundred influences of persuaders, some hidden and some more overt. Every occasion contributes something — good or ill — to his future:

memories that enrich and strengthen, challenges that have been met, friendships, atmospheres, skills. Every special occasion *can* be an enrichment of a Scout's boyhood as well as a strengthening and informing experience for his manhood. It's up to you who lead.

Chapter 15

SERVICE ACTIVITIES

When a boy becomes a Scout he makes a Promise "to help other people" and so right from the start of his time in the Scout Troop the carrying out of service is part of his Scouting Service is not an extra activity to be undertaken if there is the time; it is an integral part of the Scout programme and plays its full part in the training of the individual. Yet it is not just a selfish pursuit, as through giving service the Scout learns of the needs of others, appreciates that not everyone has the precious gift of good health, realises that there are many worse off than he is and begins to understand that all of us have a duty to help others. The Law puts it in understandable terms when it requires that — "A Scout is friendly and considerate." By helping others the Scout realises what being friendly really means and that being considerate is more than a vague feeling of sympathy for others.

The aim of Scouting is to encourage the development of young people so that they may take a constructive place in society. Service is part of our programme but we must hope to see it become an important part of a young man's life and remain so, long after he leaves the Movement, for only thus will he be taking a constructive place in our society.

A Scout is expected to be always ready to offer a helping hand, to help a child across a busy street, to pick up that piece of litter in the park and to wash up for his mother. These are good turns which are performed on the spur of the moment because of the boy's helpful nature and such actions should be encouraged not only by praise but by the personal example of the Scout Leader. The Scout Leader who cannot give a helping hand to the Cub Scout Leader when he sees her struggling with some heavy piece of equipment is not giving very much encouragement to his Scouts to be helpful in their everyday life. This chapter is not concerned with good turns but with the planned acts of service which should be an important part of the corporate life of the Patrol and the Troop and of the personal life of the Scout. The spirit which motivates a good turn is the same that lies behind a worthwhile act of service.

Service in the Scout Troop has its place in the training programme of the Scout. In the Scout Standard there are tests in the ability to help others, in the Advanced Scout Standard there are requirements in carrying out service to others and at the Chief Scout's Award stage there is a further requirement for actual service. The proficiency badges are divided into Interest, Pursuit, Service and Instructor badges and the last two types of badges encourage service both to others and to Scouts. Service is certainly no extra. It is in the very heart of all we do.

Scouts are encouraged further to give service either to the community or to younger Scouts through the Service Flash. This badge should not be easy to gain for it demands a high standard not reached by any easy path. It requires a good Scout standard, qualification to give service and the actual giving of service over a period of time. Full details are to be found in the badge and award supplement to *P.O.R.*

There are some general points which need to be made:

1. *If the service to be given requires knowledge, then Scouts should know what to do before attempting anything.* Those who want to decorate an elderly person's living room *must* know how to do the job. It is worth remembering, however, that not all worthwhile service requires training.

2. *Service does not necessarily have to involve sacrifice to be of value.* Sharing a hobby can be a service. An example is the playing of draughts with the bedridden.

3. *Do not encourage Scouts to take on commitments they cannot see through to the end.* It is better to tackle jobs which can be finished in a reasonable time rather than to accept a

continuing responsibility. The task involving a commitment of any length is best tackled by a whole Troop or even the Group.

4. *Encourage Scouts to choose service where they do not have to apologise for their youthfulness and inexperience.* Let them take on jobs where to be young and a volunteer are real advantages.

5. *Service entails actually helping other people.* To become qualified in first-aid or life-saving is training, not service. Teaching younger Scouts in first-aid or helping a spastic to swim is service.

6. *Raising funds for good causes is certainly worthwhile, but it is not the best service for Scouts.* Of course it is admirable to collect milk bottle tops, help at bazaars and deliver leaflets, but it denies the Scout the tremendous values to be found in meeting and understanding other people in his community. A Scout needs to develop his ability in personal relationships and face-to-face service provides wonderful opportunities for this.

How to find opportunities for service? The Scouts, their Patrol Leaders, and their Scout Leaders will know of some opportunities, but the openings required for service will be many. The Scouts will want jobs to enable them to qualify in the Training Scheme and this will be true of the Venture Scouts as well. In addition to these needs will be the natural wish of all Sections to give service without any thought of progress in proficiency. This all means organisation at Troop and Group level, and possibly at District level too.

Any organisation will aim to achieve two main objectives:

1. *The avoidance of a lot of members of the Movement worrying the Organisations and others who can help in providing opportunities for service.* The aim should be to help these people, not to cause them extra work.

2. *The cutting out of unnecessary delay in providing Scouts with jobs of service.* Nothing can be so frustrating for a Scout than to find his enthusiasm to take on a job met by the inability of his adult leaders to provide him with an opportunity. A Scout often gets a sudden urge to do something and we must be able to harness that enthusiasm to a job to suit his ability and time available.

What sort of Organisation might work without requiring too much administration? Within the Group itself the Leaders of the Sections working together with the Group Scout Leader and Group Council can probably cope, but it is when the service involves Organisations outside Scouting that some form of District organisation may be the answer.

This might take the form of a lay appointment of a Service Organiser who could be in touch with the various Organisations requiring help on the one hand and the Scouters on the other. It may be that the Service Organiser in the District would accept this extra responsibility. However it is done it must be done properly and preferably not by a Scouter who will have plenty to do in his Group. At all costs avoid a complicated administrative structure or any form of committee, with its inevitable meetings and discussion. A practical answer is required for a practical task.

There remain two matters to be dealt with in this chapter — *how* to find the opportunities for service and *what* jobs can be undertaken by Scouts of 11 to 16 years of age.

How to find opportunities within the community? A survey is a useful exercise in itself and will appeal to the Venture Scout Section who could do a valuable job here. The local University, College of Technology and possibly commercial companies may be prepared to advise on the carrying out of a survey. Scouts, particularly the older ones, can play a part by studying local newspapers for cases where service by members of the Movement could be of help.

There are a number of people who will be prepared to help and particularly so if they are approached by one person on behalf of the whole District. There is the Medical Officer of Health, the District Nurse, the Almoner at the local hospital and the Health Visitor. The Welfare Officer, Children's Officer and the Youth Officer may be able to suggest other opportunities. Some local Youth Committees will have an organisation to help young people to find jobs of service, and the District Service Organiser would need to be in touch with any organised body.

The local authority is not the only source. There are the local clergy, the local Council of Social Service or Rural Community Council, Women's Royal Voluntary Service, Rotary (especially their Community Service Committee) and the Salvation Army. All these are directly concerned with helping others, and Scouts can join in helping them in their valuable work.

Yet there are others who will help. The local Police may have suggestions for service and few know of what situations exist in homes better than the milkman and the postman. Many Scouts deliver newspapers and they can act as the ears and eyes of the Troop. Scouts may well find many jobs that need doing and if they cannot take them on they should let the Service Organiser know so that another Troop or Patrol can provide the helping hand.

Once it gets about that Scouts are willing to give service, many requests will come to the Movement. Soon the need to devise jobs becomes less difficult than finding Scouts and others to do them. This will underline the many opportunities to help others and the challenge must be met by a Movement which aims to play its full part in helping others in the community.

The jobs will certainly come but what is then to be done? What can Scouts tackle with every chance of doing the job well? The field is very great and here we examine some of the possibilities:

THE PHYSICALLY HANDICAPPED

Your District may have a District Extension Adviser who will be in touch with local Organisations interested in the physically handicapped, both young and old. He will be able to suggest all kinds of opportunities but one of a truly practical nature stares us all in the face. Many handicapped young people would love to be Scouts and to be members of an ordinary Scout Troop. One such boy per Patrol is enough but if most Patrols took on even that responsibility we should extend our work in this field very considerably. What a really wonderful job of Service for a Patrol of Scouts to offer companionship to a boy with a handicap. (See chapter 22.)

There are plenty of opportunities for helping the deaf, blind and disabled. Scouts can learn to "converse" with the deaf and be taught by the deaf to lip-read — a practical exercise in observation. Blind children can be taken for walks and the older person would enjoy a visit from a helpful older Scout who might take along a friendly Guide to read aloud while he busied himself in the house.

A disabled person would probably welcome help at home and in the garden. Shopping might be a frightful chore and this is something young Scouts can do and at the same time bring into a person's life the cheery chatter of young people. How often a physically handicapped person living at home just wants cheerful company and what Scouts, perhaps a Patrol, cannot provide that!

There may be a home for the physically handicapped in the area. The District Service Organiser could find out what jobs need to be done in such a place, but remember that our age range starts at 11 and many a task in a home or hospital will be more suitable for the older Scouts and Venture Scouts.

Another possible field of service is helping not the actual person handicapped but others in the home. A mother who is confined to bed for a long time would welcome help by way of taking the children out. When the husband is unable to do much in the way of gardening because of a physical disability then his wife would probably be very grateful if some of the jobs such as cutting the grass could be undertaken from time to time by a cheery group of Scouts.

The recently published *Extension Activities Handbook* is well worth buying. It costs 35p and can be obtained from the Equipment Department of The Scout Association, Churchill Industrial Estate, Lancing, Sussex.

THE MENTALLY ILL

The local Peter Pan Club for those unfortunate people who never grow up mentally would be glad of some help from the older Scouts who might join with some Venture Scouts in lending a hand. Children who are too mentally retarded to be Cub Scouts or Scouts could be involved in some activities such as a games night in the Group Headquarters. This would be a double service for not only would the children enjoy themselves but their parents would have some relief from their heavy responsibility. The local branch of the National Society for Mentally Handicapped Children would be pleased to help in making suggestions.

The Educationally Sub-Normal (ESN) child can be a Scout. The majority of ESN children live at home and many would receive real benefit by belonging to a Scout Troop. One, or at the most two, in the Troop would be enough, for they are a handful. What a wonderful service, and again not only to the boy but to his parents as well. The District Extension Adviser will make sure you get expert guidance on how to deal with these children. Boys for all their toughness are very gentle with those less able than themselves and we do our Scouts a service in bringing that better part of their nature to the surface.

THE ELDERLY

It is here among the old people that lies the greatest need. But a warning note must be sounded. There are good reasons why Scouts of 11 to 16 years of age will not always be the best people to help the elderly. The role of listener is often too passive for the Scout age group, a gardening commitment over a long period can pall, liaison with Old People's Welfare Committees can raise difficulties and to arrange for the continuity of service that the elderly need may not be easy. The last point is a vital one. It might be far better not to raise an old person's hopes only to dash them within a relatively short time when the enthusiasm to help dies away and with it the helping hand. What opportunities for helping our elderly citizens lie to hand? There is simply visiting and talking (or listening), carrying coal, chopping firewood, reading, shopping, running errands, changing library books, decorating a room or, with some Guides, going to dinner with an old person or couple — cooking the dinner first, of course!

Old people often like to get out and about. The Troop or Group could lay on a coach outing to a day in camp, put on a special performance of the Group "Gang Show," or arrange for a party of old folk to be specially entertained at a Scout display or exhibition. The elderly are often lonely and it is real service to do something with them if only an outing to some beautiful gardens.

Before any Scout Leader encourages his Scouts, particularly the younger ones, to help our older citizens, let him re-read the opening sentences in this part of the chapter. Our task is to give service not only to provide experience for our Scouts; certainly the elderly are not a section of the community best suited for experiments.

MISCELLANEOUS

There are many other opportunites. The local church may need help or a local beauty spot may need clearing of litter. There are jobs which are peculiar to a certain place or part of the country. We should keep our eyes open and see whether Scouts might have an opportunity to offer service *before* anybody asks them to do so. Observation can play its part.

OURSELVES

Scouting offers opportunities too. A Scout may not give regular help as a Cub Scout Instructor to the Pack — he has enough to do — but there will be occasions when help may be required. The Patrol Leader with time to spare in his summer holidays might help at the Pack Holiday, there may be need for spare hands at a special Pack Meeting or on an outing. If these occasional jobs come along it is the older Scouts who will give the best help; the recently joined Scout, whether up from the Pack or not, is best not used.

Headquarters buildings, whether of the Group or District, need maintaining and from time to time there will be opportunities for service by Scouts. A camp site too may need help but the long-term commitment should be avoided.

LAST THOUGHTS

Planning for service is most necessary but we must be prepared to grasp opportunities. When it snows the Troop should be ready to clear paths for those who cannot do it themselves. If the Group puts on a show, remember that entertaining old or sickly people at the local home or hospital will bring real pleasure to both the Scouts and audience alike. Our motto is "Be Prepared" — in the field of service it is essential.

Do not forget co-operation. The Patrol Leaders and their Assistants may like to co-operate with the Guides to help people. A mixed group giving service can be more effective and can be very enjoyable. Working side by side is a most successful form of mixed activity and it allows no time for shyness — there is a job to be done and doing it together is fun. The Venture Scouts, too, give service and the Patrol Leaders may like to join them on a man-sized task such as can be found in forestry, conservation and the removing of eyesores. This will have the useful side effect of introducing the older Scouts to the members of the Venture Scout Units to which they will be going in the near future.

Service is the salt that savours life; it puts into practical terms the commandment to love our neighbour; it provides opportunities of meeting and understanding others, it places responsibility on the shoulders of our Scouts; it is necessary and therefore worth doing and not least the Scout will discover that helping others is no ordinary chore for he is working for people, for the community, and he will find that it brings its own form of happiness. To the Scouter it will bring some disappointment, some frustration but much satisfaction in seeing his Scouts respond to a real need which will make the Law and Promise become real and relevant and not a dusty code to be learned and not lived.

Chapter 16

INTERNATIONAL SCOUTING

This is really rather a bad title for a chapter, for Scouting that has nothing international about it isn't real Scouting at all. One might as well talk of "Patrol System Scouting" since Scouting without the Patrol System is not the genuine article and never will be. So let's start this chapter by accepting the fact that international knowledge, training and activities are inherent in the Scout method — a normal and essential part of it that is of particular importance in this day and age.

A WORLD MOVEMENT

The very first test for the Scout Badge rightly emphasises that we are an international Movement. "Show a general knowledge of the Scout Movement and the development of world-wide Scouting" it reads, and there is no more impressive fact in our sixty years of history than the way in which Scouting literally leaped round the world to take hold in twenty-three countries between Brownsea in 1907 and the first International Scout Conference in 1922. It has gone on spreading ever since and 103 countries are now (in 1972) members of the World Scout Conference. Good Scouting is going on in very many more countries that have not yet achieved full Conference membership.

INTERNATIONAL SCOUTING

Do start your new Scout off on the right foot in his Scout career by making clear to him what it is he is joining. You will previously of course have to do a bit of research yourself to discover, if you haven't done so already, what the World Scout Brotherhood is and what it means in practice; how the Promise and Law and the Patrol System are among the basic things which bind all Scout countries together and something of what Scouting is like and is doing in other parts of the world. You'll also need to remind yourself as well as your new Scout of the positive obligation of brotherliness which is on us all as members of the World Movement, whether we be white or black, brown or yellow, Protestant or Catholic, Muslim or Hindu, Jew or Gentile. And this, of course, means a real sinking of prejudices, a determination to like and to try to understand the other chap and a belief that it's really important to do so. As each newcomer to your Troop takes his Promise you should be able to feel sure in your own mind that you have made all this as clear to him as you can and that he realises as you admit him to membership of the World Brotherhood of Scouts that he's in on a really big thing.

FRIENDS AND BROTHERS

Almost every country where there are Scouts has a Scouter at its Headquarters called the International Commissioner. His job is a big one, though it can be quite simply defined. It is to encourage, by every means in his power, personal international friendships and combined activities between the Scouts of his country and those in other lands and to work out exciting, modern ways of doing so. In Great Britain the International Commissioner is assisted in his job by a team of Assistant County Commissioners (International) throughout the country, who in turn are there to help you, the Scouter, to make World Scouting and the fourth Scout Law come alive to your Scouts. It is assumed, of course, that it has already come alive to you, otherwise you shouldn't be a Scouter at all, for if you are narrow-minded and parochial in your attitude to foreigners and to things international you are not the man to train the modern boy and you can do more harm than good. "A Scout (and even more so, a Scouter) is a brother to all Scouts." And a foreigner (a word many of us try not to use in Scouting) is after all nothing but a normal chap who doesn't happen to belong to your country or is may be, for the moment, in a country that's not his own. It doesn't need saying that you and your Scouts are foreigners to the rest of the world but whether you *feel* foreign depends on other people. If you've tried it, you'll know not only the thrill of being abroad but also the feeling of strangeness and solitariness that it can sometimes bring, as well as the joy that comes of being made to feel really welcome and at home when you're in another country. So let's never think of people from abroad as anything but potential friends and especially, of course, as Brother Scouts. This needs a bit of training and some practice and Scouting has three main ways of providing these. For ideas as to all of them you should seek out your Assistant County Commissioner (International) and it will pay you to keep in regular touch with him. Meanwhile here are a few general rules of the game.

THE WEEKLY PROGRAMME

For many a harassed Scouter this is the biggest problem in running a Troop. Ideas never seem to come when they are most wanted and when they do they are often not all that new. But the international side of Scouting offers great possibilities for programme planning and enables you to bring the wide world into your weekly training as soon as a boy becomes a Scout.

The great thing is to make internationalism a personal matter and here the Pen-Pal Scheme provides a good start. This is better run on a Patrol rather than on an individual basis so that it becomes a Patrol tradition to keep contact with its opposite number abroad. An extension of this is the Link Up Scheme whereby a whole Troop maintains a permanent relationship with a Troop in another country, swopping news and photographs of all kinds (Scout, family, local and national), Group Magazines, tape-recorded messages and songs, Christmas presents and visits.

It's never difficult in Britain, which has a long and honourable tradition of welcoming visitors and offering a home to people who have had to leave their own countries, to find someone from some other part of the world who will gladly come and tell your Scouts about his homeland. Maybe he (or she) can be prevailed upon to start an informal language group which, if kept short and light-hearted, may well help chaps who find no fun in wrestling with irregular verbs at school to realise that French or German are living languages that people really do speak. If you can catch and keep the friendly interest of a small group of such folk, you can hold periodical international Troop Nights with colour slides, films, exhibits and food from other countries and short talks about them.

Present and former Scouts and Scouters from the Commonwealth and numerous other countries come to Britain in large numbers every year. Look out for some of them to rope in to run an evening or a week-end camp for you as they would do it at home. Get your Scouts to learn and practise badge tests from other countries, to recognise their flags, to sing some of their lovely folk songs and rounds, or collect a repertoire of yells.

Scouting is different in every country where it exists. Some countries like our own and the United States have one National Association only. Others have several, divided maybe according to religion or language or the Organisation that sponsors them. Uniforms, badges, methods differ everywhere and it's only right that they should, for people and their needs and habits differ widely too.

It will be of the greatest help to the Scouter if he can keep in touch, on the adult leader level, with some of his opposite numbers in other countries, so that he can keep himself to some extent in the world Scout picture. Such contacts will enable him to pick up news and ideas, to exchange points of view and to realise that Scouts and Scout problems are much the same almost everywhere, but that there are a hundred and one different ways of dealing with them. This in itself is a consolation as well as an inspiration.

IN CAMP AND AT HOME

There's surely no better way of getting to know and like another chap than by Scouting with him. The best of all Scouting, and still by far the most popular variety, is in camp. Whether this be a Patrol Camp at a week-end, a two-man hike or the Troop Summer Camp, try whenever you can to include some Scout guests from abroad. If the Pen-Pal Scheme has really been working, or you have established a link with a Troop overseas, now is the chance for your Scouts to invite some of the boys they have been in touch with during the year. With luck the idea will come from the Scouts themselves and, indeed, it is the object of the exercise that it should do so. Then when Hans from Bremen, Sven from Stockholm, Ricky from Barbados or Hank from U.S.A., who so far have been just faces in photographs, signatures at the end of letters, or voices on a tape, actually turn up as flesh and blood Scouts at your camp, you will really feel you have achieved something. And you certainly will have done. It is probably best to invite at least two Scout visitors, or a whole Patrol if you can manage it, and let them be fully absorbed into the life of your Troop while they are with you. This means not only taking them to camp with you but fitting them into the homes of your Scouts either before or afterwards. A bit of quiet briefing of their hosts should ensure that they are treated as full members of the family, made to feel really at home, introduced to friends and relatives and shown some of the local sights. Home hospitality of this kind is one of the most important aspects of International Scouting and it can change a boy's whole idea of a country and its people. We British have the reputation of being conservative (old-fashioned is sometimes the word), stand-offish, reserved and difficult to get to know. The food we eat is regarded as odd in the extreme and is viewed with considerable distaste by most continentals. So we have something of a reputation to live down. Real Scout friendship in camp and in the home can quickly do this and there's nothing more heart-warming than a real warm-hearted British welcome. Please do your best to see that this is forthcoming. It makes all the difference.

CAMPING ABROAD

For some reason or other — probably because we're an island — it still seems to be regarded by many Scouters as terribly adventurous — even dangerous — to camp abroad at all. Planning is begun a couple of years in advance, soothing little brochures are circulated explaining to anxious parents (and are they really so anxious?) that the leader is very experienced in facing the dangers of foreign travel (he once spent a long week-end at Ostend); that the drinking water is quite safe; that every care will be taken of Tommy's health; that the Scouters' wives will be with the party to cook and wash and mend and that the site is on the French coast as near as possible to Britain. The Assistant County Commissioner (International) and the International Department at Headquarters are deluged with enquiries of every kind, though all the basic information is contained in a simple set of forms and leaflets which should be the first thing you ask for when planning a camp abroad.

Meanwhile the harrassed Scouter dashes round in a haze of organisational fervour arranging travel, obtaining passports and currency, enquiring whether tea and cornflakes can be bought locally or whether they should be carried with the party and, if so, whether they have to be declared to the Customs and, if so, what the duty is likely to be. Eventually, clad in a regrettable array of garments and weighed down with colossal rucsacs, the party sets forth. The restraints of home are abandoned; uproariousness takes hold; a studied scruffiness is assumed, for "we're going abroad."

That's an exaggerated picture, of course, but some of it has been all too true in the past. The new Design for Scouting must make it a totally untrue picture in the future. The point, of course, is to emphasise what tremendously heavy weather we are apt to make of going abroad. Just because our frontier is twenty miles of water instead of a striped barrier across a road, we tend to think of foreign travel as a major and rather risky operation, instead of the easy, normal thing it can be, and must become.

For Scouts it should be a joyous and rather special adventure certainly but also a regular part of the training cycle of the Troop. The International Commissioner at Headquarters with his colleagues in other countries, offer you, the Scout Leaders, a simple routine procedure for making your first contacts in the country which your Patrol Leaders' Council has decided on for the Troop camp. After consulting your District Commissioner, the first step is to ask your Assistant County Commissioner (International) for details of this. He will also tell you the insurance requirements and advise you generally as to your planning, if you need it. But he is not a travel agent and he will expect you and your Patrol Leaders to find out as much as you can for yourselves. He is there to start you off on the right foot, to see that you go with a clearly defined Scout purpose (not just as holiday makers in uniform) and that you have a lively, well-thought-out programme, suitable for the age range of your Scouts. When your District Com missioner is satisfied with your arrangements he will sign your P.C. (Abroad) form. The Assistant County Commissioner (International) will issue you with the International Letter of Introduction. This is the Scout Passport and is recognised by Scouts and Scouters the world over. It opens many doors to friendship.

Great Britain has the second largest Scout population in the world (the U.S.A., of course, tops the list) but has by far the largest in Europe. 12,000 and more British Scouts camp abroad each year and the number is rising. While many go further afield most go to four or five nearby and particularly popular European countries. This means that the volunteer Scouters and Commissioners in those countries, who in cheerfulness and good Scout spirit cope each year with a considerable influx of British Scouts, have a very big job on their hands. So meet them more than half-way when you can, make a personal reconnaissance of your intended site if at all possible and find out for yourself the answers to the many questions you would otherwise want to ask them. You'll find this will pay dividends all round.

And now comes what is, perhaps the most important point of all. Do see to it that your camp abroad is purposefully planned to bring your Scouts into friendly contact over a reasonable period with Scouts abroad. Those of you with some experience may well say: "But my Troop always does; we invite the local Scouts to our Camp Fires; we play them at football, and always ask them to show us the local sights and help with the shopping." Well, that's something, certainly, if perhaps a little one-sided. But it's nothing like enough. Plan to camp together with a local Troop or Patrol, if you can; Scout with them, run wide games together, hike and swim and explore with them as *you* would if *they* visited you at home. And if you can, arrange before saying "good-bye" for your Scouts to receive a few days' hospitality in local Scout homes; this can be for them one of the most valuable experiences of all.

Here, then, are ten main guide lines for you as you decide to camp abroad with your Troop.

1. **Know what you're aiming at.** A holiday — yes — but one that puts your Scouts in real touch with new people, gives them practical Scouting in excitingly different conditions, glimpses of new beauties, liking for new things, wider understanding.

2. **Plan your programme.** Let it be good Scouting in the widest sense with its quota of hiking, climbing, swimming, fishing, cooking of new food, good turns, singing, getting about in new surroundings and with new friends.

3. **Keep the parents in the picture.** They have the right to know what you are planning for their sons and can give you invaluable advice and backing.

4. **Watch the budget.** Fix a camp fee that allows for emergency expenses that perhaps you haven't thought of. It's better to make a refund at the end than to find yourself short in a crisis.

5. **Your leadership** must, of course, be exemplary. It is you who set the tone of the camp you run and of your Troop's relations with the people of your host country.

6. **Turnout and behaviour.** Set and insist on the highest standards of smartness, discipline and conduct. British Scouting will be judged by your success or failure in this.

7. **Local contacts.** Make friends not only with the Scouts but with a cross-section of other local folk, including the mayor, the clergy and the doctor and perhaps a schoolmaster, a farmer, a fisherman, a forester or a mountain guide.

8. **Go native for once.** Do some things the local way; don't just run a typical British camp abroad. There are other good ways of doing things beside our own.

9. **The language.** A bit of coaching beforehand put into practice on the spot makes a world of difference.

10. **Thanks.** Many will befriend your party. Make sure that your gratitude is shown as well as felt. A few small personal gifts brought from the U.K. and the appropriate letters of thanks sent when you get home are indispensable.

INTERNATIONAL CAMPS AND JAMBOREES

Every year a number of international camps are organised in this and other countries and Scouters should bear in mind the possibility of occasionally taking their Troops to one of these. They are always fun; they offer a variety of unusual activities in the company of Scouts of different nationalities and almost always include a period of home hospitality. Details of invitations of this kind can be obtained from your Assistant County Commissioner (International).

The greatest international Scout gathering of all — the World Jamboree — is held every four years. This may well be up to 20,000 strong, with Scouts from anything up to a hundred countries taking part. Competition for places is intense and it is for the Venture Scout rather than the Scout section of the Movement. To attend a World Jamboree is one of the thrills of a lifetime for it shows a Scout, as nothing else can, that he is indeed part of an immense and unique World Brotherhood. We cannot but be proud that that Brotherhood, through B.-P.'s genius, had its origin here, and determined always to give of our best to ensure its highest fulfilment.

BOOKS TO READ

The following book will give you more ideas for activities. (Available from Scout Shops):

Ideas for International Scouting (The Scouter's Books, No. 27).

Chapter 17

RELATIONSHIPS WITH OTHER PEOPLE

A long and proud history can be a help; it may also be a burden. The Movement's many years have given it respectability, authority and a unique position among those Organisations working for youth. But, our detractors shout, they have also led us into being isolationist, smug and self-centred.

Let us by all means preserve our good qualities. The others must go, for with them we cannot flourish. Despite our unique position, we must recognise that our training is part of and not separate from other forms of youth training — in short, our Movement is part of the country's Youth service; its work is complementary to that of other Organisations. On no other grounds than success in applying our training programme and ideals do we deserve respect.

We must set about achieving this success with all the means at our disposal. Those we have already may not be enough. Running a Troop on a shoe-string may have been possible — and satisfactory — in less affluent days. Today, boys are more demanding; they are not willing to put up with the merely second best — and neither are their parents. If boys find their Scouting is provided in a leaky hut magnetic to all stray draughts, a hut prevented from falling down only by the woodworm holding hands, then they will look elsewhere for their pleasures. If the tents are cotton sieves and the pioneering ropes are salvaged sisal; if the income is barely more than the threepence a week from each boy, then we haven't a version of modern Scouting which we should or our boys will tolerate any longer. We need to present a public image of sleek, deliberate efficiency. A kindly but wayward and a near-bankrupt amateurism is incongruous side by side with authority-sponsored professionalism — a quality seen ever more clearly in the nation's Youth Service.

THE YOUTH SERVICE AND SCOUTING

One sure way to give ourselves a modern image is to play a bigger role in the Youth Service. A business-like co-operation can only be beneficial. In many areas we are at cross-purposes with the Youth Service, if its existence is recognised at all. We misunderstand it, and we in our turn are misunderstood. But, remember, we are both working for youth; we want and aim to provide a programme which is not in uneasy competition with those of local Youth Clubs and Associations. What their leaders are doing is, no more, no less, as important and necessary as is our work.

The Youth Service is usually directly associated with the Local Education Authority. The exact nature of the Service will vary from one Authority's area to the next, but the aim is always the same—to help youth. It provides courses in youth leadership, training facilities, grants for training courses, leaders for the Youth Organisations under its control and places for these Organisations to meet. It achieves all this by using public funds. It may also administer the allotting of grants for building purposes. For these reasons alone, it is hard to imagine why many District Scout Councils don't have a representative on their nearest Youth Service Committee. Why soldier on, making do, mending, merely getting by, when near at hand may be the means for avoiding much of the penny-scraping that goes on in the Movement?

The Youth Service realises the importance of the vast amount of research being made into youth leadership. It should go without saying that many of its courses are of the greatest potential benefit to Scouters. Places on them should be sought avidly, for with our emphasis on training in practical activities we need to study the theories and experience of those whose field work with youth has been outside Scouting. No doubt, too, our ideas would be welcome. Ours is the widest experience in outdoor, adventure training. Our Patrol System, camping methods, emphasis on service — all must give others not associated with Scouting much from which to draw ideas and inspiration. Is there one logical reason, untinged by emotion, why we shouldn't be represented on the local Youth Service Committee?

THE TROOP AND ITS NEIGHBOURS

Isolationism in Scouting is usually very basic. It is to be found not so much in the District as in the Troop. This isolationism springs from pride, pride in the Troop's history or traditions, or merely because it is called the 3rd Wigglesworth (Pilchard's Own) and not the 4th Wigglesworth (St. Michael and All Angels).

A Scout, it must be said, derives great benefit from being able to identify himself with a unit he can understand and feel part of, and for these reasons the Troop is viable. But he is done a grave disservice if isolationism becomes a fad and an end to be desired above all else. Its dangers are manifold. Scouts are denied contact with others of the same interests, aims and hopes. They are denied the opportunities which only the District, in co-operation with other Troops, can provide. They are denied the benefits that come from sharing equipment and resources. They are denied the security that comes from one Troop helping the next. Their Troop may, in the end, emulate the pelican which plucked its heart out to feed its young.

So, as with the Youth Service, there is everything to be gained from co-operation with other Troops. To co-operate is to strengthen; to isolate is to weaken.

In many closely-knit urban areas there is obvious benefit to be gained from the pooling of resources; Groups with low numbers, poor financial standing, inadequate equipment, few Scouters, are not providing Scouting of the quality we need. Together, they could put one decent-sized Headquarters to full use; improvements in quantity and quality of equipment could be made; black bankruptcy would no longer threaten their very existence. And we would get one very important priority right: Scout Leaders would be more free to lead Scouts. Today the

Scouter spends too much of his time a mendicant vulture gratefully picking up money where and how he can. The burden of money-earning must be lifted from his shoulders; it is the job of others to fill the coffers.

Scouting was never meant to pester man: it should be a game. Rationalisation will help keep it so. If there is an obvious case for pooling, then with all speed go about it. You, your Scouts, the District, Scouting will benefit. We are too inclined to be content with the status quo; we are reluctant to stir up local sensibilities, but careful, diplomatic handling will cause good sense to prevail.

There's no doubt that Scouts will enjoy and derive great benefit from all forms of inter-Troop activity. Scout Leaders have for their inspiration the new Training Programme and this will naturally be the basis for both indoor and outdoor activity. Its uses are boundless. Co-operation between Troops will enable experiment after experiment to be tried when, previously, they were quite beyond consideration. One Troop might have canoes, another nylon climbing-ropes, a third pot-holing equipment. It's not likely that each will be using its specific equipment every week-end. How much more sensible it would be for Groups to let each other know what they have and are prepared to lend. In a very short time there will be the means for many to try what previously was open only to the few.

Groups, too, have their experts in various fields or know whom to ask to help them in certain activities. These people are more comprehensively and economically used when they teach not only their own Group's keen climbers, skin-divers and canoeists. By sharing, lending and borrowing, our service to Scouts will be more likely to reach another aim — to give to as *many* as want it as *much* as we can of Scouting's richness.

As Scouts grow older, their interests develop and widen. They will still regard the Troop as their base, as home. Nevertheless, we should hope to awaken in all an ever more enquiring mind, sparked into life by imaginative and original activities undertaken both inside and outside the Troop. That assumption which says that this or that activity will not interest the Scouts is both illogical and based on wilful ignorance.

In all fields of work and pleasure there are experts who are willing to help open your Scouts' minds. Local government officers, doctors, veterinary surgeons, coroners — all can lead discussions on their work; men of achievement will tell of their exploits; industrial firms and public corporations will allow visits; the legal system is open for all to see in the Courts. In all of society there are men who realise the importance of letting youth see what lies ahead and will give their services to lift the curtain a little. One of Scouting's aims has ever been to fit its Scouts for responsible adult life. Those who deliberately orientate their programmes so that every Scout increasingly realises as he grows older that he is expected to be a responsible citizen will be doing the Scout, society and the Movement a service.

MIXED ACTIVITIES

It is surely a mistake to force mixed activities on a Troop which has little real desire for them. This does not mean, however, that we should neglect opportunities for introducing activities in which Scouts and Guides would naturally take part. To introduce a discussion on mixed activities is always to stir up a hornets' nest. The range of biases, bigotries and prejudices revealed is wide enough to satisfy the keenest fancier of subjective argument. On the one hand will be the advocates for the application of the Law of Equal Misery which states that what they haven't had nobody else may have either. They will find bedfellows among, strangely, those preaching monasticism. And in opposition will be the equally emotional get-them-together-at-all-costs faction. Good sense ought to prevail, but in many cases it won't. Laughed to scorn, ridiculed, those preaching moderation will sit and wonder.

Their case must, eventually, win. They realise that there is much of our respective programmes which is most effectively and efficiently carried out separately. To mix, in these circumstances, would be artificial. Yet, as Scouts grow older, they increasingly want the company of girls and they may express a desire to have some joint activities. Such a desire should be anticipated by the imaginative Scout Leader and he should be ready to introduce into the programme dances, discussion groups, joint training courses and the like.

To make any or all of these activities a success, co-operation with local Guide Companies is of prime importance. It will be necessary to build a relationship based on confidence. Planning must be thorough and the aim behind the proposed mixed activities properly determined. These requirements satisfied, mixed activities will play their proper part in a Troop's programme.

COUNTY AND DISTRICT EVENTS

Programme planning is often approached in an *ad hoc* fashion, a regrettable course. The Scout Leader who follows it, harried as he may be by all around him, is further plagued with the prospect of filling in his Scouts' time for a number of hours a week, and his gratitude is boundless when there flies into his mind relief in the form of any idea or scheme with which to defeat the clock.

The trouble is that programme material derived and adopted in a piecemeal fashion may not be what is required. No element of selection has been imposed. The principle ever is: get an idea and apply it. Forceful and thriving Counties are cornucopiae of ideas, and for their success they depend on Troop support. From all sides you are pressed by invitations, exhortations and fulsome behests. In a season there may be a comprehensive à la carte menu of camping competitions, cooking festivals and handicraft expositions. The District meanwhile lets it be known that it expects your undying and unswerving devotion at swimming galas, Gang Shows, sports days, numerous other competitions, and all laced with compulsory attendance at marches and parades to celebrate the annual recurrence of this day and that.

Good programmer or not, stop and think awhile before you say yes to requests for your Troop's support at all or some of the above. You have a Troop to run, a Troop with its own necessary ties of loyalty, service and progressive training scheme. What, perplexed as you are, must you do? The answer is: select.

All things being equal, if the choice is between a Patrol Leaders' Training Camp and a District Wide Game, the first must win every time. If the Troop is planning a highly adventurous night hike and the County's annual woodwork show clashes with it, there is, in my respectful judgement, no clash. The Troop's programme must take priority.

County and District events must, then, be examined under a very critical eye. Ask of all of them if they will merely disrupt the Troop's programme or if they will create new interest; if they will give a zestful incentive to the Troop or if they will fill in gaps in the training scheme, gaps you, for various reasons, cannot or are unwilling to close. Negative answers mean ignore them — and people will respect your reasons.

To be considered apart are training courses. The District and County are able, because of their infinitely greater resources, to provide experts and facilities for teaching and learning far beyond most Troops' capacity. Moreover, not only does a Scout learn something new by attending but he also meets his peers from other Troops. There is a worthwhile interchange of ideas, opinions and experiences, and the result, a wiser Scout who has had a new social experience, well justifying his absence from the Troop.

NATIONAL EVENTS

National events — the Explorer Belt scheme and the Scout Car races are two popular examples — have a special appeal. If there is a real keenness in Scouts to take part, and if the exercise will help generate enthusiasm in particular elements of the training programme, then Scouts should be given the opportunity to take part. In any case, to take part may add that necessary spice and novelty to normal Troop events. For this sensible reason alone they deserve consideration for a place in your Troop's calendar.

DUKE OF EDINBURGH'S AWARD SCHEME

The scheme has a great appeal to Scouts. It recommends itself to the Movement on these grounds: all three stages — Bronze, Silver and Gold — encourage participants to take an interest in those very activities and pursuits we are trying to foster in our own training programme. Yet one doesn't make the other redundant. The Award Scheme, for example, places great emphasis on the exercise of personal initiative and on the acceptance of an obligation to serve others — qualities we hope to develop in Scouting. Scouts who are encouraged to take part in the Scheme will be the better trained Scouts for it. If we want to train forward-looking, enterprising, adventure-seeking, responsible Scouts, the Duke of Edinburgh's Award Scheme will help us. (See chapter 23.)

Of all the old Scout Laws, probably 'A Scout is a friend to all and a brother to every other Scout no matter to what country, class or creed the other may belong' was the one most honoured in the breach than in the performance — at least at Troop level. To replace this Law we now have 'A Scout is a brother to all Scouts' and 'A Scout is friendly and considerate.' What the first means to Scout Leaders we have already discussed. The second also applies to much of what has been said. But it has a more general implication. It encourages us to continue friendly relationships already formed. It obliges us to extend and develop them. It asks us to open new ones.

What we can offer others must govern all our relationships. This being so, inside the Movement, Troop Scouting will benefit. Outside the Movement our aim to be of service will be seen to be a fact. The respect in which we are held will climb; our public image will be one to be proud of; we shall be admired for training boys in ways of good citizenship. The development and encouragement of sympathetic relationships, then, is of prime importance to the Movement. After all, as John Donne said: "No man is an island, entire of itself; every man is a piece of the continent, a part of the main."

Chapter 18

TROOP ADMINISTRATION

DISCIPLINE

In Scouting, as in any community, good discipline is essential if progress is to be made and a happy Troop is to be built up. Ultimately boys appreciate it: they soon tire of an ill-disciplined free-for-all, and have no respect for the leader who allows it.

The basis of Scout discipline is self-control. Your Scouts should carry out your instructions because they want to do so, not because you have ordered them to do so.

Your greatest ally will be a good Troop tradition. This can be built up only by a quiet but firm insistence on high standards from the very beginning of your leadership. Once it is established, many orders and instructions will no longer need to be given: the right things will happen because "we do it that way in this Troop."

Issue instructions in a firm tone that expects obedience; you are then much more likely to get it. Keep them brief and clear: if they are at all elaborate they are better written on cards and handed to Patrol Leaders.

You must be able to get silence quickly, and for this an easily recognised "freeze" signal should be devised. This may be a distinctive whistle, but should not be a shout from you: shouting leaders produce shouting boys. Insist on silence during the issuing of oral instructions.

Games should have a smart start and finish, and the rules

once established must be observed. Any Scout who insists on breaking them can become a spectator.

Punctuality is an important part of Troop discipline. Start Troop meetings on time, exclude latecomers from the opening ceremony, and require explanations from them later.

You must be prepared to check slackness at once. If possible, avoid reproving a boy in front of others. In minor matters, you may be able to get his Patrol Leader to speak to him. More serious matters you must deal with yourself. Try to convince the boy that although you disapprove of his conduct you do not dislike *him*. This calls for great tact, and good humour.

Keep punishment to an absolute minimum, and never threaten any action unless you fully intend to carry it out if necessary. Never use fatigues, such as sweeping the Troop Room or washing up in camp, as punishments; if you do so, tasks which should be honourable service to the community will be debased into chores to be shirked. Avoid sarcasm at all costs. If at all times you maintain your respect for the personality of the individual boy, he will respect you as his Leader.

UNIFORM

Uniform will be worn on all formal occasions, which include District and Group parades and other events at which the Scout Movement is on view to the public, and the Troop ceremonies discussed in the next section.

Uniform should also be regarded as normal wear for most other occasions; in fact it should be worn unless an activity is planned for which it is clearly unsuitable. In that case the guiding principle is that the dress most appropriate to the activity should be worn.

If a meeting is entirely or largely devoted to a strenuous activity, such as rock climbing or a wide game, the appropriate "activity dress" will be old clothes, and uniform will not be worn at all. Shorts and plimsolls remain the most generally useful wear in camp, but the Troop should be in uniform on the journeys and outside the camp.

It is your responsibility as Scout Leader to see that your Scouts wear uniform of the correct material, colour and style as specified by Headquarters, and that their parents know where it can be bought. Incorrect imitations of Scout uniform can be kept off the market only by Scout Leaders refusing to accept them in their Troops.

Encourage your Scouts to take a pride in keeping their uniform smart and wearing it correctly. They should come to and from Troop meetings in uniform. No member of the Movement should be unwilling to be seen in public in Scout uniform.

Note that, in the Scout section, the long-sleeved pullover and the outer garment are integral parts of the uniform, not optional extras. Scouts can therefore be in uniform and yet be adequately clothed in cold or unsettled weather. In continuous or heavy rain a cape or raincoat may be needed.

Every Scout must have a green beret, which is an item of standard uniform. However, it need not always be worn with uniform. It will be for the Scout Leader to decide whether headgear is to be worn or not at a Troop activity. The outdoor activity during a Troop Meeting and an expedition or outing from camp are occasions when the beret need not be worn and yet the Scout will be in correct uniform. Headgear should be worn on formal Troop occasions or on those public occasions when full uniform is advisable in order to present a good appearance. It is important that at collective events where more than one Group or Section of the Group is present, there is a common policy for the wearing of headgear.

Inspection of uniform need not take place every week: probably at irregular intervals of two or three weeks, and without warning, is about right. Never accept "I hadn't time to change into uniform" as an excuse: changing takes about five minutes, and this can always be found if the will is there.

CEREMONIES

Scouts undoubtedly like a measure of ceremonial and tradition, but they are rightly sceptical of meaningless ceremony and traditions which have no relevance today. Ceremonies should therefore be reduced to a minimum, and should be short, simple and sincere. Boys cannot remain solemn for long, so don't overstrain their patience.

An outdoor setting is desirable, if a suitable time and place can be found. All those taking part should be carefully briefed beforehand, so that they are confident that they know what to do.

Coming-up from the Cub Scout Pack

If possible the Pack and the Troop should meet together. The Pack bids a simple farewell to its members, who are then welcomed into the Troop by the Scout Leader, and to their new Patrols by the Patrol Leaders.

Investiture, or the making of the Scout Promise

This is the most important of all Scout ceremonies, and should be conducted according to the following suggested pattern.

The Patrol Leader conducts the boy to the Scout Leader. The boy is then asked if he knows the Scout Law and repeats the Scout Promise phrase by phrase after the Scout Leader. He is then presented with his badges and given a brief explanation of their meaning. The ceremony is rarely improved by additions. Elaborate ritual with the Troop Flag, for instance, is quite unnecessary: the Scout promises *on his honour*, making the Scout Sign to signify this, and these should be sufficient tokens of sincerity.

Investitures should not be held immediately after strenuous activity. The best time is at the start of the meeting, when everyone is fresh. The Investiture may then be followed by an appropriate short prayer. The alternative, but perhaps less satisfactory, time is at the end of the meeting, just before closing prayers.

The Investiture is a very personal occasion for the Scout, his Scout Leader and the Troop: he is making a solemn promise, and they are going to help him to keep it. It should therefore be conducted by the Scout Leader, not by a visiting Commissioner, however exalted. Scouts should be invested singly, never *en masse*. If you must invest several on the same occasion, take one or two at the start of the meeting and one or two at the end. Put the Troop at ease for a few moments between the individual Investitures. This ceremony should never be made into a public display; the parents of the Scout to be invested may however be invited.

Installation of a Patrol Leader

The Scout Leader asks "Are you prepared to undertake the

responsibility of leading the .... Patrol?" and perhaps also "Will you undertake to do your best to put your Patrol before yourself, to put the Troop before your Patrol, and to be a Scout worth following at all times?" It may then be appropriate for the new Patrol Leader to renew his Scout Promise (possibly from memory now) in token of his acceptance of his responsibilities.

Going-up to the Venture Scout Unit

If the Group has its own Unit a joint meeting may be practicable. But if the Scout is going up to a Unit shared with other Groups, the Troop should simply bid him farewell, with thanks for his past service and good wishes for his future Scouting. It should be borne in mind, however, that Scouts who join Venture Scout Units which are organised on a local basis may well see fit to seek qualification in the service requirements of their Award scheme by acting as Instructors in the Pack or Troop of their old Group.

Presentation of Awards and Proficiency Badges

It is a pleasant tradition for a Troop to have its own form of cheers or yell to express its congratulations.

Flag Ceremony

This forms an appropriate start and finish to meetings at which uniform is worn. Fly the flag outdoors whenever possible. Train your Troop to move quietly; parade-ground stamping is out-of-place in Scouting. It is incorrect to salute a flag when it is lowered; the Troop may however salute at the moment of dismissal, as a gesture of farewell. If flags are carried on a formal parade, correct flag etiquette must be observed, and every detail be adequately rehearsed beforehand.

. . . .

These are the only ceremonies which are needed in the Scout Troop. Do not allow frivolous or childish additions to them. So-called initiation ceremonies at camp should be forbidden: a Scout camping for the first time is often sufficiently ill-at-ease already, and the practice is open to serious abuse.

RECORDS

Properly kept records are of great value to the smooth running of the Troop, and are essential if a change of Scout Leader takes place or your equipment store is burnt down.

Your main concern as Scout Leader is with your boys and their progress, so you will be well advised to hand over to others as much record-keeping as possible. But there are two or three things you must look after yourself. These are:

(1) A file for correspondence, which should be sifted annually. Camp papers should all be kept: they will be invaluable if you re-visit the same site.

(2) A notebook, in which you record the programme of each meeting, and what was achieved. Absentees should be noted.

(3) Possibly also a loose-leaf book, with a page for each Scout, for personal notes which could not appropriately be recorded in the record and progress file.

The record and progress file should be kept up-to-date by your Assistant Scout Leader. It contains a card for each Scout, on which are recorded his personal details, his progress through the Training Scheme, and his camps and expeditions. Progress may, in addition, be shown on Troop or Patrol charts displayed in the Troop Room; and every Scout should have his own Progress Book. All these items are obtainable from the Scout Shops.

The Troop account book, recording subscriptions received and expenditure met from them, can be kept by another Assistant Scout Leader appointed as Treasurer. If subscriptions are collected through Patrol Leaders, they may keep Patrol attendance and subscription registers.

The equipment stock book should be kept by an Assistant Scout Leader, an Administrator, or an older Scout appointed as Troop Quartermaster, who must carry out an annual stock-taking.

The Patrol Leaders' Council will appoint a Secretary to record the minutes of its meetings. This is good training in committee procedure.

Finally, Patrol and Troop logs, if properly kept, are an invaluable record of the Troop's history. Appoint a methodical Scout, not necessarily a Patrol Leader, as keeper of the log, and let him encourage as many members of the Troop as possible to contribute to it. At the very least, do keep illustrated logs of every camp and expedition: they will be a joy to re-read in later years.

EQUIPMENT

You cannot run a Troop properly without adequate equipment, so a vigorous effort must be made to acquire it. It can conveniently be divided into four categories. The suggested lists are not exhaustive:

Patrol training equipment:

Each Scout should possess *The Scout Handbook*.
The Patrol Leader's Handbook (held by the Patrol Leader).
A selection of other books.
Writing and drawing materials.
Maps: (a) local Ordnance Survey 1-inch and 2½-inch.
(b) local street maps.
Compasses, Silva type recommended.
First-aid kit, suitable for Patrol hikes. (If possible, have a kit for practice also.)
60ft. of ¾in. circ. braided lifeline.
Ropes, 1-inch circ., one per Scout.
Whipping thread.
Handaxe in case.

(There are further suggestions regarding Patrol training equipment in *The Patrol Leader's Handbook*.)

These are kept in a locked Patrol box, and supervised by the Patrol Quartermaster. It should be inspected regularly. You have spare keys to all the Patrol boxes on a ring, and can come to the rescue when necessary.

Troop training equipment:

More specialised books.
Silva or prismatic compasses.
Pressure stoves.
Pioneering gear: spars, lashings, ropes, blocks.
Games equipment.
Tools; e.g. hammer, saws.
Flags.

These are kept in a central store, and supervised by the Group Quartermaster, who may be an older Scout, an Assistant Scout Leader or an Administrator.

Patrol camping equipment:

Patrol tent. (This may well be held as Group gear.)
Hike tent.
Lath table top.
Dining shelter.
Chest containing a set of cooking equipment.
These are also kept in the central store, but are supervised by the Patrol Quartermaster, the Patrol being responsible for their maintenance. Either you or the Group Quartermaster should inspect them periodically.

Group camping equipment:

Other tents, for Scouters, stores, etc.
Latrine screens.
Other cooking gear.
Lanterns.
Further tools.
First-aid chest.

These are kept in the central store, and supervised by the Group Quartermaster.

FINANCE

The two main sources of income are your Scouts' own subscriptions, and Group funds, in the raising of which the Scouts should also have played some part, through Bob-a-Job Week, for example.

Subscriptions must be in keeping with present-day values; a reasonable amount is probably between sixpence and one shilling per week. Weekly collection is time-consuming; the calendar month is a better period. Quarterly collection may appear better still, but probably results in parents footing the entire bill. Scouts should be encouraged to pay their subscriptions out of their own pocket money.

Subscriptions may be collected by Patrol Leaders and handed on to the Troop Treasurer, who keeps the accounts and sends them to the Group Treasurer annually.

Expenditure to be met from this fund will include secretarial expenses, meeting expenses, and the purchase of badges.

for which the recipients should not have to pay directly. The fees of Scouts taking training courses may be partly met by grants from Troop funds. They should also cover the routine repair and replacement of Troop and Patrol equipment. Allocation of money to Patrols for this purpose should be discussed by the Patrol Leaders' Council, which thus checks the good husbandry of the Patrol Quartermasters.

Alternatively, regular allocations may be made to Patrols from Troop funds. If so, the use to which these are put should be periodically checked by the Scout Leader and the Patrol Leaders' Council.

Patrol subscriptions and funds (in addition to the Troop ones) are of doubtful value, since they may put an undue financial burden on the members of one Patrol. It is better for Patrol Leaders to put their needs before the Patrol Leaders' Council: this keeps a salutary check on extravagance.

Group funds will be called on for the original purchase of camping gear, and for the replacement of major items such as tents.

The finances of camps and expeditions should be kept separate, and each should be self-supporting. Fix an amply adequate fee: it is better to make a refund afterwards than to ask for a further payment. Offer financial assistance from Group funds to any Scout finding special difficulty in raising the camp fee, but expect him to earn and save as much as he can.

Chapter 19

ADULT ASSISTANCE

Your success or failure as a Scouter may well depend on your handling of colleagues. You cannot run a Scout Troop single-handed, neither should you want or need to try. The wise Scout Leader is like "The Reluctant Gardener" who thinks hard before doing anything and never does anything if someone else could do it instead. First plan your programme and then plan the help you have got so that you can complete that programme. Remember the Patrol Leaders in their Council do the planning, guided by you in the background and either Scouts or your adult Assistants do the work. This leaves you free to do your proper job of future planning, training the Patrol Leaders, co-ordinating help and encouraging your Scouts' parents.

ASSISTANT LEADERS

Assistant Scouter Leaders may either be Permit Holders or Leader Warrant Holders. If Permit Holders they will be new recruits and will be in the process of doing their basic training and you should pay extra attention to encouraging their progress and to helping ease them into taking an active part in the Troop programme. Try and remember what you felt like when you started and give them good warning before asking them to do anything in front of Scouts.

It can be very embarrassing for an adult to be "shown up" in front of those he is trying to train, but it is especially so when he is new to his job. Be patient, therefore, and be prepared to discuss and guide in all the small details which go to make up Troop training and tradition. Your reward is in seeing your Assistant grow in confidence and usefulness. Of course your Temporary Leader Permit Holder may have come straight from the Venture Scout Section or may have been a Scout a while back. In this case, your job will be a little more simple, but not much. There is all the difference in the world between being a Scout Leader in a Troop and being a Patrol Leader or on the Executive Committee of a Venture Scout Unit. Therefore, the new Leader must have this explained to him right at the beginning. His job is now like the wind which encourages the windmill to turn and grind the corn whereas, before, he was the windmill itself.

Your Assistant Leader may, on the other hand, be a Leader Warrant Holder and have completed his basic training and may also have undertaken his Advanced (Wood Badge) training. In either case, it is important that this is not considered final and the chance of taking additional courses must not be overlooked. The Assistant Leaders will do your job while you are away on training or for holidays; there should be help available for this purpose within the District as well, if needed.

Assistant Leaders are thus the foundation of a good Troop and help to provide the continuity, knowledge, support and inspiration needed in the real training of Scouts. In some Troops the Assistant Leaders will help particularly with some of the more strenuous activity training and adventure, but in all Troops they will be needed to help the Leader in charge of the Troop in some particular responsibility and should be told quite clearly what this is.

INSTRUCTORS

Instructors will also be in two categories: those who are regular helpers and those who help occasionally. Regular Instructors need a letter of appointment from the District, but even occasional Instructors need the approval of the District Commissioner, although no formal appointment is involved.

Regular Instructors may well be those who are just out of the Venture Scout Section and who wish to help in the Troop but have not the time or inclination to take on the job of a

Scout Leader. Alternatively, the job can well be done by someone who is willing to help, but who does not wish to become too deeply involved in the organisation and training of Scouts.

The regular Instructor is not required to do any training, although he may, of course, do so if he wishes.

Occasional Instructors are essential to help in some of the more complex training, such as karting, photography, radio, geology, car maintenance, conjuring, judo, etc.: the list is endless. Some of these skills will have to be taught away from the Troop where the specialist equipment is to be found, or in the correct environment. Scout Leaders will find they need considerable help from such experts in the training of their Scouts to make sure that they can follow the hobbies of their choice. It is impossible for a Scout Leader to know all about these subjects and he must not try to become the proverbial "One Man Band." Anyway, this is now out of fashion and it's the generation of the Group!

BADGE EXAMINERS

Badge Examiners for the proficiency badges in the Pursuit, Service and Instructor groups will be appointed by the District and may cover several Groups or even a whole District. You are responsible for arranging examinations for proficiency badges in the Interest group, although the District may well help by providing a list of people prepared to do this work. Remember that the Badge Examiner will not normally be needed for testing the Scout Badge, Scout Standard or Advanced Scout Standard, which are all passed by the Scout Leader or Patrol Leader. The only exception will be if a Scout wants to take a proficiency badge which then qualifies him for part of his Progress Badge. Badge Examiners will be reminded on appointment that it is the effort involved which goes a long way to qualify a Scout for a badge, provided of course that any basic standard set is attained. Scout Leaders are also asked to make sure that Badge Examiners know when they are to be asked to examine and that Scouts do keep the arranged time.

THE VENTURE SCOUT SECTION

The Venture Scout Section may be a source of help to a Scout Leader. Both the Venture Award and the Queen's Scout Award require regular service and this may be undertaken within the Movement. It will be worth while keeping in close touch with your Venture Scout Leader, even if this is a Unit not attached to the Group, so that you can help each other. Venture Scouts can, for instance, help maintain equipment or buildings, act as Instructors or even help with transport if properly qualified.

ADMINISTRATORS AND LAY HELPERS

Once again the unloading of work is part of the art of doing the job of Scout Leader properly. You will find it a great help to get a layman to do much of the routine work involved in running a Scout Troop, such as the Uniform fund, the supply of uniform, Quartermaster, Information Officer, and possibly to help keep the Troop records or as Treasurer or Auditor of Troop funds, Clerk of the Works responsible for the site at Headquarters, etc. Many of these jobs may be undertaken at Group level and, of course, the Group Scout Leader and the Group Scouters' Meeting would decide what is wanted. Lay help is an *essential* part of the adult assistance for a Troop and the time taken organising this help will certainly be well worth while.

DISTRICT SERVICE TEAM

It may be that some of your lay helpers may wish to be part of the uniformed side of the Movement, and if so, may join the District Service Team. They will then be registered by the District but may give their committed service in any way they choose and to any part of the Movement. This service can be given as an individual or in conjunction with other members of the Team. The minimum age limit of members of the District Service Team is 18 and the upper age limit normally 65.

The District Service Team may also be useful to hold those leaving the Venture Scout Section who do not wish to take up any other appointment. The amount of service done is not specified, provided a genuine commitment is made.

PUBLIC AND PARENTS

Are "they" really necessary? The answer is: "Of course"; that you would not only be out of business without them, but also that you cannot manage without them. Scout training is only part of life; parents, school and the general public make up the rest of the environment of your Scouts. Parents should be told what is going on in the Group (Group letter?) and their *active* co-operation as supporters is very desirable. Parents must also be consulted at all stages in the Scout's career so that they may encourage their sons to progress and, anyway, the more parents are told what is happening the more they will trust Scout Leaders and support them in their work.

The public are also necessary to the Scout Leaders for financial and practical help but, not least, for indulgent understanding of the tasks undertaken.

It is then plain that no Scout Leader can hope to be doing his job to the full if he is not helped at every point by Assistant Leaders, Instructors and the community as a whole. They will all ease the burden of a Leader and so help him better to enjoy his job of training his Patrol Leaders.

THE B.-P. SCOUT GUILD

The B.-P. Scout Guild came into being twenty years ago. One of the main objects of this Guild is to assist the uniformed Movement. Invariably branches of the Guild, where they are in existence, include ex-Scouts who have a considerable experience of life and specialist knowledge which covers a wide field. The members of this Guild wish to be used in forwarding the interests of Scouts and we strongly recommend that they should be called upon as much as possible. Here, then, is yet another important source of Adult Assistance which is available — and a willing one too.

Chapter 20

TRAINING FOR THE JOB

If, having read the previous chapters, you have concluded that there's nothing very much to the Leader's job, then read on! This chapter is especially for you!

If, on the other hand, you appreciate that the job is demanding and complex and that you will assuredly need help and training, then there's something here for you, too!

Much has been spoken and written of the arts of leadership — and that it is fundamentally an art and not an applied science, let there be no doubt. But all art needs development and guidance. None of our great leaders of the past ever came to their fulfilment without a great deal of training and experience in their earlier and formative years. In all humility, then, let us believe that in each one of us there are latent possibilities which, if developed, will fit us to take our place as a good leader in our chosen sphere — but only if we really make the effort.

Let us keep before us this basic principle:

"Leadership is the art of effective persuasion."

How, then, can we become 'effective persuaders'? This really comes in two complementary stages:

(1) We can do a great deal of self-training.

(2) We can profit from the experience of others.

To a large extent we can regard the first as Informal Training, and the second as Formal Training. Let us then take a look at these in some more detail!

INFORMAL TRAINING

In a way all life's experiences are informal training to the extent that it takes an old man to acknowledge that he has still much to learn, both of life itself and of his own trade or profession. Our objective must be so to direct our time that we gain a residue of profitable experience from our recreations and activities, which will help us in our job of Scout Leadership.

Quite simply, we won't learn an awful lot by accident.

And so we need some reasonably careful planning of our spare time so that what we do brings new knowledge, new understanding, new ideas and wider horizons to the ultimate benefit of our leadership and to the boys whom we have been privileged to lead.

A few examples will probably suggest many more — and they are not in any order of precedence.

1. Reading

Obviously a vast amount of man's knowledge is gained from reading, and this is equally true in the field of youth training. While the technical and semi-technical books and pamphlets in the range published by The Scout Association cover a great deal of ground, much can be gained from publications dealing in a wider sense with the Youth Service as a whole. Recommended books are reviewed periodically in *The Scouter* and a list can always be obtained from your Assistant County Commissioner (Leader Training) or from your Local Education Authority Youth Organiser.

Apart from all that, *The Scouter* is a most valuable source of reference for up-to-date news and ideas. For the Leader it is really 'required reading.'

To read widely, however, on general subjects is as important — biography, travel, history — leaving the novel or "who-dun-it" as perhaps a rarer treat than it is now!

Much, too, can be learned from the veritable spate of magazines, pamphlets, journals and articles which are produced by kindred Organisations and Youth Service authorities. And one must not forget the newspapers — particularly the Sunday "heavies" — where many relevant contributions are to be found with a good deal of well-pointed comment on our own methods and organisation.

2. Hobbies

This is rather an old-fashioned word, but one which embraces our own special and spare-time interests. Everyone needs some alternative interest to his daily work — and it is a great mistake to assume that your work as a Scout Leader is just another hobby. It is much more than that. So, if we are good with our hands we find relaxation and pleasure in some manipulative skill; if we have artistic leanings we turn to something creative; and lacking either we may turn to a new intellectual pursuit.

The Leader who has a hobby interest in, say, photography, gardening, fishing, handcrafts, art, music, etc., is bound to gain from these material assistance to his leadership. Opportunities abound in most areas to develop a wide range of hobbies through Evening Classes run by the Local Education Authority, and there are, of course, many Clubs and Societies which provide guidance and tuition to their members.

A Scout Leader really should have a hobby, if only to help balance his enthusiasm. We all know how abrasive the single-minded enthusiast can be in his relations with others.

3. Activities

One is probably drawing rather fine distinctions in seeking to differentiate these from hobbies, but they are referred to here as those interests where the participant has, in general, to exercise some degree of physical skill and effort. Many of these lie close to the heart of Scouting, and without a considerable leavening from what are essentially specialist activities, Scouting would be a dull and stodgy lump.

One thinks here of the traditional outdoor activities first — mountaineering, orienteering, rock-climbing, canoeing, sailing, ski-ing. In each and all of these, abundant opportunity exists to learn as a beginner from courses run by specialist Bodies: the Central and Scottish Councils of Physical Recreation, and, increasingly, one hopes, Scout-sponsored courses. Then there is swimming, water-skiing, skin-diving, if one's tastes turn to water-borne activity.

Less common, perhaps, because they are a little more expensive are pony-trekking, kart-racing, scrambling, rally-driving, caving, gliding. etc.

No reasonably fit person is ever too old to learn one of

these. It cannot be too fully realised that most youngsters only find their interests channelled into an activity because of the persuasion and guidance of some adult who himself is a participant. You do not need to be an expert to introduce Scouts to an activity but it is an inestimable advantage to have a good working acquaintance with it. The expert can take over where you leave off, but the important factor is that an activity should be introduced attractively and competently, with due regard to costs, suitable equipment, special clothing, safety measures, best localities, etc. Upon that depends a little more than just a nodding acquaintanceship on your part.

It is, then, fair to say that a Scout Leader should have reasonable competence in at least one activity — the joys and rewards will come to you personally as much as to your Scouts.

4. Interests

These might be classed as those things which take somewhat less time, concentration and, perhaps, money, than a hobby or activity. It might be something taken up for a short spell —say, a winter or summer season — yet something which leaves behind a rich residue of experience.

Such things as bird-watching, zoology, geology, forestry, conservation, collecting — all have their relevance and, indeed, may well develop in themselves to be fascinating and lifelong hobbies.

These, then, are some of the ways which can be explored to provide a fund of knowledge, expertise and a widening of horizons informally, and largely outside Scouting, but which will prove invaluable to the Leader.

FORMAL TRAINING

This side of training is that which is specifically and directly brought to the aid of the Leader in an organised way, perhaps by planned courses and activities, either exclusively Scout, or alternatively Youth Service or allied courses. Let us first look at what the Movement itself provides!

The Past

Training is nothing new in the Movement — it has been provided on formal lines now for the better part of 50 years, ever since our Founder evolved his novel and unique scheme of Wood Badge training for Scouters. It is well to realise that in this, as in many other things, Scouting was far in advance of other Youth Organisations in its provision for the training of its leaders. Many have only recently entered this field. Perhaps the main criticism of the system was that only the volunteer who offered himself was trained and a large number of Leaders passed through the Movement without ever having contact with a formal training course.

The Future

In future, no Leader will be confirmed in his appointment unless he has completed a prescribed course of Basic training. When a Leader is first appointed he is issued with a Temporary Leader Permit, which allows him to work as a Leader under probation for a period of up to two years, but no longer. At any time during this period the Basic training can be completed, and then the Leader will be confirmed in his appointment.

The next stage of training is the Advanced (Wood Badge) training, which all Commissioners, Group and Section Leaders must complete within a period of five years of confirmation of the appointment. Otherwise the appointment is terminated.

Assistant Leaders, who also require to undertake basic training prior to confirmation of appointment, are, however, not obliged to complete Advanced (Wood Badge) training in any prescribed time. Nothing, however, prevents an Assistant Leader commencing Advanced (Wood Badge) training as soon as he is confirmed in appointment, and it is anticipated that many will wish to do so.

Instructors and Administrators are not placed under any obligations so far as formal training is concerned, but they may, if they wish, complete both Basic and Advanced training.

The Organisation of Scout Training

Scout Leader training is the responsibility at national level of the Director of Leader Training and Camp Chief of Gilwell Park. Each Scout County, or perhaps group of Counties, has, in its turn, an Assistant County Commissioner in charge of the Leader Training in his own County. These Commissioners have a staff of experienced Assistants who will have special knowledge of one or more of the Sections of the Movement.

Nationally, an agreed syllabus is prepared for every course so that in point of content, presentation and duration, every course held in the United Kingdom, be it at Gilwell Park or John o' Groats, is the same so far as basic and Advanced training is concerned. At District level it is the responsibility of the District Commissioner that an adequate number of courses of training are available for Leaders under training. In practice this responsibility will be discharged in general by an Assistant District Commissioner (Leader Training).

Location of Scout Training Courses

Basic training courses will, in the main, be organised at local level by the Assistant County Commissioner (Leader Training) and will be held at a suitable local centre. While it is hoped that such courses will be run at reasonable frequency, because it is necessary always to have certain minimum numbers of candidates, there may be at times a rather long interval between succeeding courses. In such cases, and indeed at any time, there is nothing to prevent a Leader attending a course in an area other than his own.

Advanced Leader Training courses, which are arranged at National level, are usually held either at Gilwell Park or at a Training Centre. Other suitable centres may, however, be used from time to time in order to meet a special or local demand. The dates and locations of all Training Courses are available from Gilwell Park.

The Content of Basic Courses

Obviously, as this course is the potential Leader's first introduction to the complexities of his task, the course will deal fairly extensively with fundamental matters. These include such things as the basic organisation of the Movement, its methods, its guiding principles, its religious policy. Basic instruction in some of the technical skills will be given and these will be considered in their relevance to the programme of Scout training.

Current educational techniques and a consideration of their adaptability to Scout training will be dealt with. A general introduction will be given to the work of the Youth Service as a whole. Not least, will be an opportunity to consider the boy in his environment, his attitudes to society as a whole and the social pressures bearing on his development.

The Content of Advanced Courses

While the obligatory course deals only with the basic and minimum requirements of the Leader, the Advanced course carries on, and develops from this to a consideration, in greater depth, of some of the matters only lightly dealt with in the obligatory course. The course will relate these to practical situations provided in the general context of work in the Scout Troop. Programme planning will loom fairly largely throughout the exposition of the section programme as a progressive and practical reality. Candidates on the course will be able to participate in a variety of Scout Troop activities.

In addition to attendance at a practical course the Leader will also require to carry out a period of prescribed personal study in his own time, and to produce written evidence of these studies in a correspondence with tutorial advisers drawn from the Training Team.

Finally, having completed both practical course and theoretical study, a period of satisfactory "in-service" application in the Leader's own unit will ensue before the District Commissioner recommends the award of the Wood Badge (Advanced Leader Training Emblem).

The Wood Badge scheme of training is, of course, international and Leader Trainers (Deputy Camp Chiefs) are regarded as members of the International Gilwell Training Team. Wood Badge training is currently operating in more than 130 countries, and the inter-change of trainers between countries is encouraged in order to spread the unifying influence of Scouter training throughout the world. There is, too, a World Training Advisory Committee which, amongst many other functions, has to make sure that the minimum standards which are acceptable for Wood Badge training are maintained in every country.

Duration of Scout Leaders Courses

Basic courses may be arranged in a variety of ways — by a series of evening meetings, by whole-day meetings, by residential week-ends or week-ends under camp conditions. The choice is left to the Leader Trainer in charge of the course, who will tailor his course to suit the convenience of most of the candidates. All courses will provide the same minimum number of hours of training.

The practical course of Advanced training normally extends over a period of seven days on continuous courses, or over three long week-ends.

Other Scout Leader Courses

In addition to courses run for the Leaders of the other Sections, and for Commissioners of Sections, numbers of specialist and technical courses are organised and run on a national syllabus. These include:

Courses on the Promise and Law, which have special relevance to the place of religion in the Movement.

Courses in Scout administration.

Courses in Extension Activities.

Courses on specific parts of the Section training scheme.

Your County will, in addition to the above, probably arrange and run a variety of short courses on certain aspects of your job, which may, on account of the time factor, only have been lightly touched on during basic and Advanced training. These would certainly include courses on camping standards, catering, cooking, first-aid and rescue, games and expeditions, etc.

Formal training from agencies outside the Movement

Most Leaders, particularly those living in the large urban areas, will have ample opportunity to attend courses run by Local Education Authorities and Youth Service agencies, and much of the content of these excellent courses will be found extremely useful and relevant. Again, the specialist bodies such as the British Red Cross, St. John and St. Andrew's Ambulance Associations, Adventure Training Centres, the Central and Scottish Councils of Physical Recreation, run many courses on their specialities at a variety of centres. In most of these a certificate of competence can be gained in whatever skill or technicality has been pursued. It goes without saying that such courses train to a much more advanced level in their subjects than that reached in general Scout courses.

Paying for Training

The cost of training should not fall wholly on the candidate.

While it may be reasonable to expect people to pay something to cover the cost of their food, no-one need be prevented from undertaking training because he cannot afford it. Many Local Education Authorities will provide up to 100% grants to cover the cost of prescribed courses, while others may only provide a proportion of the cost.

Counties and Districts, too, make arrangements to cover these expenses and your Assistant District Commissioner (Leader Training) will help and guide you in this matter.

Local courses are generally inexpensive and the charge is usually only sufficient to defray the cost of food.

ADDITIONAL AIDS TO TRAINING

One important aid to training for the job must not be overlooked and that is the enormous help and assistance the new Leader will obtain from a period of attachment to a well-run Troop under an experienced Leader. Most District Commissioners treat this as an early part of the training process and the new Leader will probably find that he spends the first two or three months of his service away from the Troop in which he is to serve. This is a most valuable experience and tends at once to give a wider outlook and base on which to build than would be the case if all service were to be continuous in the Group in which one perhaps started as a boy.

The Programme and Training Department at Headquarters will also provide, on request, valuable assistance in the shape of programme ideas and methods.

Your own County or District will also have, or be building up, stocks of training-aids in the shape of models, charts, films, etc., called visual aids: many of these can be purchased or, in the case of firms, hired from agencies acting on behalf of Headquarters. (See chapter on "Training Aids").

TO SUMMARIZE

What you will need — and what you can get — to make you an effective Leader will, or should, include:

1. Self-help — reading, observation, study.
2. Attachment to another Troop.
3. A course of Basic training.

4. Participation in a Youth Service course.
5. Participation in specialist courses run by County, District, or outside agency.
6. Use of the Movement's resources — films, charts, visual aids.
7. Organised personal study for the Wood Badge.
8. Attendance at a practical Advanced Leader Training course.
9. Application of what has been learnt.

A formidable list, you say! But remember all this is to be done over a period and indeed, as we said earlier, the good Leader will never cease throughout his service to seek opportunities for learning and training.

Above all, let us remember that there is nothing fundamentally difficult which prevents the average chap becoming a good Leader. The opportunities are there — skilled trainers, specialists to help and advise. All that it needs is the will to learn and a determination to absorb and retain what is available.

Throughout the ages genius has always been in short supply, so that most achievement in the world has been, and always will be, the work of painstaking, ordinary individuals. Let us caution ourselves, therefore, against believing that we are born leaders and need no-one's help, but comfort ourselves by the thought that we, too, can make the grade as a good Leader — if we but try!

Chapter 21

SEA AND WATER ACTIVITIES FOR ALL SCOUTS

The Sea Scout Supplement included in this Handbook is directed particularly to Sea Scout Leaders because of the special nature of the training programme of their branch. The Sea Training Programme, which is supplementary to the Scout Progress Scheme, is intended to be followed as a pattern of training by all Sea Scout Troops. The progressive standards of efficiency and the adventure activities incorporated in the Sea badges are intended to match the physical development of Sea Scouts starting training at the age of about 11.

Nonetheless, the Sea Training Programme is open to all Scouts, no matter what their ages, who wish to reach recognised standards of proficiency in sea activities. This chapter is intended for the Leaders and Instructors in non-Sea Scout Troops who have to organise their training. They will, of course, find much in the Sea Scout supplement which will be useful to them. (Chapter 24).

The most difficult problem is likely to be the provision of adequate instruction. Equipment is likely to be different from and less plentiful than that used by most Sea Scout Troops. Above all, whereas the Sea Scout will probably start his training at about 11, other Scouts will probably not turn their interest to water activities until much later, say at 14 or even

15, although canoeing may become an attraction earlier.

The Sea Activities Committee for your District or County has as one of its responsibilities the promotion of sea activities for all Scouts. The Committee should be approached as soon as the need arises for information on what equipment and training facilities are available.

Provided, then, that the facilities are available, perhaps with the help of a Sea Scout Troop, boys showing an interest in sea activities should be encouraged to obtain the Boatman Badge as quickly as possible. Having completed this basic but quite comprehensive stage, some will branch off to a particular water activity related to local opportunities, e.g. dinghy sailing on a reservoir. Others who show a more general bias towards the sea should be encouraged to attempt the further stages of the Sea Training Programme. The syllabus as illustrated in the Sea Scout Supplement provides ample material in itself for a lively plan of activity afloat.

Whether the particular interest is canoeing, rowing, sailing, power craft operation or any other, the provision of courses is probably even more important for Scouts than for Sea Scouts, because they will be trying to reach the standard in a relatively short time. Advantage should be taken of approved courses arranged by Organisations such as the Central Council of Physical Recreation and the British Canoe Union, where no Scout-organised course is available.

Leaders faced with the problem of providing suitable craft for Troop needs will probably find the hard-chine and double-chine kit-constructed type of boat better suited to their needs than the larger, more traditional boats required by a Sea Scout Troop for more general purposes and extended activity.

Because canoes are cheap and easily made at home, they are well suited to inland waters such as gravel pits, streams and smaller rivers, and make ideal vehicles for interesting and unusual Scoutcraft journeys, and any Scout Leader may be faced with a suggestion that the Troop should "do something with canoes." The canoeist proficiency badge has been specifically designed to meet that demand.

The rules about swimming qualification, the use of life-jackets and other boating rules are equally applicable to Scouts and Sea Scouts. Before undertaking canoeing as a Scout activity, the advice of the local Sea Activities Committee should be obtained. It is important to remember that efficiency in water activities is essential to the safety of those taking part. An adequate level of skill must, therefore, be insisted on as a condition for taking part in any extended water activity.

There will be cases where the formation of Sea Scout Patrols within ordinary Scout Groups has to be considered to meet the interests and demands of a section of the Troop. The District Commissioner, after consultation with his Sea Activities Committee, must decide whether this is desirable. A change to Sea Scout uniform is only to be recommended where there are suitably qualified Instructors available to provide adequate specialised training and continuity for such Patrols. In this connection, Leaders and Instructors associated with ordinary Scout Troops are reminded that any course which includes sea activities is open to them. Indeed, they are more than welcome to participate whether the course be at an Activity Centre or sponsored by some other recognised Organisation.

Chapter 22

EXTENSION ACTIVITIES

The term Extension Activities embraces Scouting for boys with handicaps. It covers, as the title suggests, activities for Scouts, and their planning and implementation, which will sometimes necessitate an extension of the basic principles involved in dealing with normal boys. This will be necessary in order to make them suitable, absorbing, worthwhile and enjoyable, to boys who are physically or mentally handicapped, but who are at the same time capable of understanding the Law and Promise.

We should recognise that, although a boy may be handicapped in limb or mind, he is still a boy, and that when he is given Scouting he becomes a Scout, not a handicapped Scout or an Extension Scout.

Before giving a lead as to the sort of things one should know about as they may affect Scouting for the boy with a handicap in your Troop, District or County, a brief word concerning the organisation of the Extension Activities Branch of Scouting and its purpose.

HOW THE EXTENSION BRANCH IS ORGANISED

The National Extension Activities Board, with the Headquarters Commissioner for Extension Activities as Chairman and a member of the Headquarters staff as Secretary, meets at least twice a year.

EXTENSION ACTIVITIES BOARD — ITS PURPOSE

It is responsible to the Programme and Training sub-Committee of the Committee of the Council for:

1. Advising the Movement on training and activities for *Scouts* in the Extension Branch.
2. Keeping abreast of medical thought and practice so that the Movement may be up-to-date in its methods and techniques.
3. Development of Extension Activities.
4. Forming personal contact between Headquarters, the Movement, and specialists concerned with the training of handicapped children.
5. Carrying out any functions delegated to the Board by the Programme and Training sub-Committee.

The Extension Activities Board comprises members drawn from Scout Leaders holding various appointments from each of the Scout Regions in England and from Scotland, Northern Ireland and Wales. Also lay persons and specialists in education, medicine, welfare, etc.

Information concerning Extension Activities and regular news of the Branch, which will assist Scout Leaders in giving Scouting to boys with a handicap is given in SCOUTING and from time to time in Extension Bulletins. You can help other Leaders to spread interest within the Branch and within the Movement as a whole by sending to the Programme and Training Department of Headquarters notes of games, training aids, sources of lay help, camps, expeditions, etc., and news of special challenges and how these are being met.

HOW TO FIND BOYS WITH A HANDICAP

Some will seek and find *you*. But the majority, because of their disabilities and shyness and their restricted mobility, will depend upon the interest and enthusiasm of others to introduce them to Scouting.

Who? you may ask. Well, first their friends who are Scouts: then by spreading the news of the possibilities of Scouting for the handicapped in conversations which lead to contacts with parents. Other proven sources are almoners at hospitals; ministers of the church; the various welfare Societies and

Borough or County Welfare Departments. This can be done best, though, through people who are interested enough to become District Extension Advisers and who, possibly through specialist training, will have acquired knowledge of the various Societies whose special interest is the welfare of handicapped children. Our interest, of course, is Scouting, not solely welfare.

The District Adviser will arrange liaison with the local Borough Welfare or Education Department and Special schools, thus opening up the potential of the handicapped boy at school.

Occasionally a boy may be transferred from a Troop in another District, and a Transfer Form will reach you, which will give particulars of his *Scout* history and a brief word concerning his handicap. This is quite a standard form, which is available for use throughout the Movement and requires the attention of the Scout Leader both in regard to its prompt origination at the one end, and speedy action at the other.

The County Extension Adviser will be working at County level, making and maintaining contact with the County Education Authority and, possibly, the County Medical Authority, and he will find and train suitable District Advisers, after consultation with the District Commissioners.

Some County authorities are prepared to contact parents of children with handicaps and inform them about the facilities within the County for their sons to become Scouts. Usually the replies from the parents are passed via the head teachers to the County Extension Adviser or to the local District Adviser.

Other County authorities are willing to pass to the County Adviser lists of school children with handicaps for direct contact by the County Adviser and the District Adviser. More co-operation in this regard is needed. It must be remembered that all information concerning children which is passed to the Scout Movement is confidential.

A further extension of our Scouting is in regard to spotting handicapped boys in wheel-chairs, in the street or in the park, when it may be possible to make direct contact with the boy *and* his "pusher," who may be a member of his family.

To further the work of the Extension Branch, it is possible to obtain a complete list of all Department of Education and

Science recognised schools and institutions, This includes all those schools, institutions, hospitals and centres which are officially recognised by the Government Department as being efficient and also private institutions.

HOW TO DEAL WITH BOYS WITH A HANDICAP IN THE TROOP

If you are a Scout Leader in a Troop with one or more handicapped members, you may feel hesitant in facing up to the possibilities of Scouting for the boy with a handicap *in your Troop.*

For years it has been the Movement's policy to encourage the integration of children with handicaps into normal society and particularly in regard to Scouting. Even at Cub Scout age this is not too early, and Scouting which was designed for boys — all boys — makes the integration of the handicapped with the non-handicapped possible *and*, in a *normal* activity, not one that was created especially for the handicapped.

Being handicapped often entails living with a deformity, and the sense of belonging to a normal activity such as Scouting can contribute tremendously to the well-being and happiness of such a boy.

Scouting has made thousands upon thousands of boyhoods better and happier. Although not every boy will wish to face up to the obligations of Scouting, there is a worthwhile challenge open to the boy with a handicap, and to his able-bodied brothers in the Movement, which the precept of the Scout Law and Promise encourages. And where there is encouragement, with your help, a measure of achievement will, or should, result.

There are limitations to what a boy with a handicap will be able to do as a Scout and he himself is aware of these. "British Bulldog," for instance, will be a spectacle rather than a personal rough-and-tumble to remember, for he knows that boisterous games or activities which need physical stamina may be beyond his present capabilities. What matters is that quiet encouragement and opportunity should be given in regard to what he *can* do rather than what he cannot.

How will he fit into your Troop programme? First, he will be a member of a Patrol and participate wherever possible in its activities and outings. If it is possible there should be one or two other boys with a handicap in the Troop. Because of his handicap he may have more time at home to practise the skills and to dream up "free scope" activities for his Patrol. He may have to be pushed in his wheel-chair in order to reach his Scout Headquarters and outdoor activities, but this is merely living up to the 4th and 5th Scout Laws.

In dealing particularly with a Scout in a wheel-chair, it should be borne in mind that, on arrival at Troop Meetings or outdoor activities, he will first wish to *see* what is going on and then, whenever possible, to *do* the same sort of thing that the other Scouts are doing. He may not be able to manipulate his wheel-chair without help and his personal attentions in regard to toilet, etc., should be anticipated. It is really a matter of common sense.

All that you do to meet the expectancy and hopes of the rest of the Troop will be just as interesting and meaningful to him. The essential elements of Scouting: reliability; personal contact; progress; belonging to a Patrol; the Troop ceremonial and discipline; the fun and friendship; display; exploring; and, within limits, competition; all these things concern *him* and will be a part of his anticipation. Like the other members of your Troop, he is a Scout with his own characteristics and idiosyncracies.

Your District Extension Adviser will help you further in regard to the provision of suitable assistance for boys with a handicap in your Troop and also in supervising the standards to be attained by individual Scouts.

If you are a Scout Leader in an Extension Troop, your daily job may entail working with boys with a handicap. In that case you will already have faced up to their needs and you may rather wish to know more about the Scouting that takes place in ordinary Troops. Inviting the District Extension Adviser to your Troop Meetings will be of value to him and may also provide a complementary link for you both to visit other Troops in the District.

In all Extension activities, the aim should be to provide normal Scouting, extending the programme where necessary to fit the needs of boys with a handicap. This should be done within the laid down standards of the Movement and without disrupting the overall plan of the Troop. Remember that each boy is an individual.

Scouts who are handicapped wear the standard Scout uniform, but the make-up of the garments may need minor modifications to facilitate ease in dressing for individual boys. For example, fully buttoned or zipped shirt fronts.

Any need for major adaptions to meet the essential requirements of certain boys should be referred to Headquarters. However, wherever possible, it is in the best interest of the boy who is handicapped to retain the same image as for other Scouts in the District.

There are no special badges or insignia for wear by Scouts in the Extension Branch.

There is no individual registration of boys with a handicap in Scout Groups, but all Scouts who come within the aegis of the Government classifications of handicap are shown in the census returns each year.

THE EFFECT OF BOYS WITH A HANDICAP ON THE NON-HANDICAPPED

With the help of the Scout Law a real Scout will accept a handicapped boy like any other boy.

Scouting can give a boy with a handicap opportunities for proper attitudes and inter-personal relationships with other boys. These will help him, and them, to deal with the realities of life and to prepare both for the life that they will have to meet when they leave school. The non-handicapped boy will grow up used to having handicapped people around without the embarrassment one sometimes sees.

STANDARDS

Just as there are minimum standards for Scout Troops there must be equivalent standards for Extension Groups and, where necessary, for boys with a handicap in ordinary Troops. But the Scout Badge is the basic requirement for membership for everyone and it must be recognised that anything less is unacceptable, whether handicapped or not.

It follows that "educationally sub-normal" boys who will not in other ways be able to reach the peak of progress in Scouting, are required in order to qualify for membership of the Movement, to meet the requirements laid down for the Scout Badge.

The minimum standards set for Scout Troops are referred to elsewhere and, wherever possible, the Extension Branch will aim to observe these, for a boy with a handicap will really want to measure up to the standard of his Troop, if he possibly can.

He, too, will want to experience a feeling of achievement and, therefore, should not be allowed to "skate" round any obstacles or to have the test "watered down" for him. Any equivalent requirements should provide equal challenge and need the same amount of effort as the normal tests. These should also meet the same purpose with the same expectancy of success.

Whilst boys with handicaps should be encouraged to meet the normal requirements of the Scout Progress Scheme, where it is not possible for them to do so in a reasonable time, or where it would aggravate a particular handicap, the District Extension Adviser will assist in regard to the standards to be attained by individual Scouts.

A special minimum standard applicable to an Extension Group is prescribed by Headquarters on registration, having regard to the nature of the handicap of members of the Group.

The standard age ranges apply to Scouts and Leaders.

CLASSIFICATION OF HANDICAPS

The activities of the Extension Branch cover all the handicaps, except the "mentally sub-normal," listed by the Department of Education and Science.

These are: blind; partially sighted; deaf; partially deaf; diabetic; epileptic; maladjusted; delicate; physically handicapped; speech defects; dual or multiple handicaps; educationally sub-normal.

Advice concerning the general aspects of the different types of handicap and the particular problems, needs, methods of education and physical limitations associated with them, is given at Special Training Courses for Scout Leaders and for Extension Advisers. Other important techniques such as moving, lifting, personal help and wheel-chair manipulating and lifting, are also included in these courses.

SCOUT MEMBERSHIP OF BOYS WITH A HANDICAP

Where it is possible to do so without detriment to other children, many children with handicaps today are absorbed into ordinary schools, and although numbers of such children are also segregated in special schools, medical opinion favours the handicapped child being allowed to lead as normal a life as possible.

We in Scouting want to help in this way and in doing so we must be efficient in our Scouting and in our dealings with local Educational and Medical authorities and also with parents. We must be seen to be efficient and to have the necessary qualifications acceptable to the authorities.

Our policy is to integrate, where possible, members of the Branch into ordinary Scout Groups and to provide assistance for Scout Leaders who have handicapped boys in their Troops.

CAMPING AND OUTDOOR ACTIVITIES

Camping under normal Troop camp arrangements may be inadvisable for certain types and degrees of handicap, but Extension Camps planned and run on a County or Regional basis, with ample tentage and adequate facilities for toilet and baths, and also indoor accommodation for those who, for medical reasons are not allowed to sleep in tents, have proved successful.

Your District Extension Adviser or County Extension Adviser will be able to advise you further, and particulars of recommended requirements for these camps may be obtained from Headquarters.

Outdoor activities can be made easier for boys with handicaps by the use of cars or a minibus, and members of the B.-P. Scout Guild will often co-operate in such a service. Remember, though, to contact them in good time when such services are likely to be required.

Boys with handicaps are just as interested in a quest for adventure as are ordinary boys and, even if some cannot participate in the actual activity, they will enjoy the planning and wherever possible and within their capabilities they should be given an opportunity to participate. Let them, for instance, be brought to the mid-way or finishing rendezvous and given a chance to help there.

Boys in wheel-chairs can go on hikes, accompanied by a capable "pusher," or on a Patrol boating exploration. Swimming, also, is often beneficial to them, but check first with the parents and obtain their permission. You will, in any case, know the boy's parents, for both they and the boy himself can help you so much in making him a regular member of your Troop.

Rough ground is hard on leg callipers and on wheel-chairs and you will find a repair tool kit a useful item of outdoor activity equipment.

Participation in games will sometimes be limited because these are beyond their physical abilities. But they themselves know their limitations and can assist with scoring or, when competent to do so, act as umpire. Most of them can blow a whistle as hard as the next boy!

Explanation of training games will interest a boy with a handicap even if he cannot take an active part in all of them.

With ingenuity, and sometimes by 'handicapping' the non-handicapped to provide equality of action, useful results will be obtained. One hand for tying a bowline and the like is but one example. You might have an occasional session of games biased on this basis, the ideas coming from the Scouts.

THE NEXT STAGE

After the Scout training stage, there is the possibility for boys with handicaps to progress into Venture Scout Units and thus enter the final stage of their training for taking their place in society and "standing on their own feet."

You, the Scout Leader, will have served him well if, throughout the years he has been in your Troop, he accepts his handicap, although not easy for him, and decides to go on from there.

Despite all that can be done for the handicapped, their way through life is likely to be hard, and they need encouragement to be self-reliant, optimistic in outlook, hard working and, as far as possible, skilled.

By now they will know of the possibilities for service to others, and in the future as adults (when they must be treated as such) some may become Leaders, and others members of the B.-P. Scout Guild. This all because their period of Scout training was thorough and because you, their Scout Leader, was so painstaking.

We conclude with a phrase uttered by General Sir Rob Lockhart when he was Deputy Chief Scout and to which you can fit your own story —

"That's not a burden; that's my brother."

ESSENTIAL READING

The Extension Activities Handbook, published by The Scout Association at 35p, obtainable from The Equipment Department, The Scout Association, Churchill Industrial Estate, Lancing, Sussex.

Chapter 23

THE DUKE OF EDINBURGH'S AWARD

Since 1960 The Scout Association has been an Operating Authority for this Award Scheme which bears the name of the Duke of Edinburgh, well-known for his personal and active interest in young people. The Award Scheme, with its emphasis on service, pursuits, physical fitness and exploration, has an affinity with Scouting which makes it attractive to members of the Movement. The Scheme is available to both boys and girls at school, in industry and in Youth Organisations. Because of its range of 14 to 21, it can form a further link between the Scout Troop and the Venture Scout Unit.

There are three Awards — Bronze, Silver and Gold. For those who gain them there is a special lapel badge and a certificate. The certificates for the Gold Award are normally presented by Prince Philip at special receptions held for the purpose.

Members of the Movement may work for all three Awards but it is permitted to enter the Award Scheme at any of the three levels without having gained the previous stage. Details of the method by which Scouts may gain the Awards are set out in the leaflet on the Duke of Edinburgh's Award Scheme obtainable from Headquarters. This leaflet also lists Award

Scheme literature which may be obtained from the local Youth Office.

The age requirements governing direct entry are as follows:

Bronze Award:
minimum of 14th birthday.
Silver Award:
minimum of 15th birthday.
Gold Award:
minimum of 16th birthday.

The Awards must be gained within the following age limits:

Bronze Award:
minimum of 14½ years — maximum of 21st birthday.
Silver Award:
minimum of 15½ years — maximum of 21st birthday.
Gold Award:
minimum of 17th birthday — maximum of 21st birthday.

Scouts may enter the Award Scheme at either the Bronze or Silver level. Those who enter at the Bronze level should achieve the Bronze Award while in the Scout Troop. Any Scout in the Award Scheme going up to the Venture Scout Unit should have gained or be aiming at the Silver Award.

To enter for the Award under the auspices of Scouting, a Record Book must be purchased from an authorised source. This may be Headquarters, a National Headquarters, the County or the District, according to local arrangements. In any case of difficulty a letter to Headquarters will provide the answer.

The Scout may enter the Scheme at school or through another Organisation but the conditions are exactly the same. Some of his achievements as a Scout will be accepted by the Local Education Authority or his Youth Leader, just as the Scout Leader may accept outside qualifications for progress in the Scout Training Scheme.

There is a very important rule of the Duke of Edinburgh's Award Scheme which must be remembered by all Scout Leaders. No retrospective qualifications are permitted, so the Scout who wishes to qualify for the Bronze or Silver Award in parallel with his Scouting progress must enter at an early date and not wait until after gaining his Advanced Scout

Standard, Chief Scout's Award or any proficiency badges. Planning is necessary by both the Scout and his Scout Leader or any advantage of using Scouting qualifications for the Award, or vice versa, will be lost.

The assessors for the various sections of the Bronze and Silver Awards must be approved, as follows:

Bronze Award:
by the Group Scout Leader;
Silver Award:
by the District Commissioner or an Assistant District Commissioner, appointed by him for the purpose.

An assessor may be a Scouter or lay man such as a Badge Examiner, but he need not be a member of the Movement. The important point is that they should know the subject concerned and where appropriate be qualified. This is no more than we demand of our own Examiners.

The Bronze, Silver and Gold Awards have to be made by different authorities in Scouting. The Record Book will have to be sent to the right person when completed for any of the three Awards. The right person in each case will normally be —

Bronze Award:
District Commissioner or an Assistant District Commissioner appointed by him for the purpose.
Silver Award:
County Commissioner or an Assistant County Commissioner appointed by him for the purpose.
Gold Award:
Headquarters of The Scout Association.

In most Local Education Authority areas there is a local Duke of Edinburgh's Award panel. If there are many Scouts and Venture Scouts in the Award Scheme then there will probably be a Scout member on the panel. The panel is there to help and if you want assistance do not hesitate to ask for it. The panel is not a controlling body but it does keep an eye open for too wide a variation in standards.

Special arrangements exist for Scouts in the Extension Branch; consideration can be given to an application for extra time where good reasons exist; and possible qualifications can be approved where doubts exist. If you have any problems which cannot be solved locally you should write to Headquarters, who will be happy to help. Headquarters is the Operating Authority and all queries should be sent to the Programme and Training Department and not to the Duke of Edinburgh's Award office.

Chapter 24

SEA SCOUT SUPPLEMENT

(including notes for the guidance of Leaders of Scout Groups undertaking water activities)

MAKING USE OF WATER IN SCOUTING

In Great Britain no boy lives far from water of some sort, whether it be pond, dyke, lake, river, or the sea itself. Not all this water is available for boats or swimming, but there are still hundreds of miles of inland waters where craft can be operated. Where there is a foot of water, there is depth enough for a canoe or punt.

It is also true to say that wherever there is a stretch of water, boys will be attracted to it sooner or later. And probably sooner! Home-built rafts appear, fashioned often with Heath-Robinson skill out of every sort of material. The spirit of adventure seems to be roused in boys more readily by the presence of a stretch of water than by anything else. In these modern times, Scouting activities may sometimes seem artificial in the sense that fast cars and coaches are passing the camp site continuously. A cinema may be in sight on the horizon. A power pylon may even be standing near the wood where Scouts are cooking on an open fire. But afloat one seems supremely unconscious of such things. A few hours in a boat takes a boy into a new world and gives him a sense of achievement. Stepping into a boat has the scent of adventure; going away single-handed or, later, in charge of a crew is adventure itself.

Offering these attractions, it is natural that water should play a major part in Scout activities. More particularly is this true for a Sea Scout.

AIMS AND PRINCIPLES

Sea Scouting is an integral part of the Scout Movement governed by its general policy, aims and principles. A Sea Scout is one who has chosen to do his boating and other sea activities in the context of Scouting. It is his special pride that his training includes all aspects of woodcraft as well as skills afloat. Water should, therefore, be used as a background for developing his Scoutcraft ashore, which in turn should be integrated with his activities afloat. Cruising in boats, combined with camping out, features so prominently in Sea Scout training that Scoutcraft training is of prime importance.

Sea Scouting, like all Scouting, is concerned with training and developing the characters of Scouts. Sea Scout Leaders use both water and land as means to their end of producing good men able to think and act constructively in the service of others. It is not our job to train and produce future admirals or master mariners. Nonetheless, the training we give must not fall short of the standards of efficiency necessary to enable our Scouts to undertake their adventurous activities with reasonable safety to themselves and their companions.

A Sea Scout learns, practises and uses his Scouting skills on or about the water, usually in boats; and he should do so right from the start. Going afloat is never 'make-believe' and must not be taken too light-heartedly. Where the water is more than a foot or two deep, there is always an element of risk; where there are tides or currents, weirs, sandbanks or rocks, the degree of risk becomes substantial. So, whether we are using the open sea, estuary, lake or inland waterway, the need for competency and a sense of responsibility in all who use the water remains the same. As Leaders we must make sure that we develop these qualities in ourselves by training and practice and instil them in our Scouts by example and training.

Not every Scout who wants to row, canoe or sail wants to, or indeed can, be a Sea Scout. And he does not have to be one. The Sea Training Programme can be followed by any Scout who can get the necessary instruction. If he wants to build his own canoe, his Scouters should see that he gets the best possible advice both on how to build it and afterwards on how to use it on the water.

Finally, of course, your Scouts must be encouraged to swim and swim well.

THE TRAINING PLAN

The Training Programme for Sea Scouts is designed to run parallel to the main training scheme for all Scouts. Covering as it does the whole age range of the Scout Section, the Sea Training Programme is framed to run in standards of achievement as follows:

Scout	**Sea Scout**
Scout Standard	Boatman Badge
Advanced Scout Standard	Coxswain's Mate Badge
Chief Scout's Award	Coxswain's Badge.

The Programme is also designed to provide a common aim and purpose for each of these three badges, the *ability to give service afloat.*

The syllabus of each badge is broken down into three stages:

Boatman Badge	–	Preparation
		Practice
		Project
Coxswain's Mate Badge	–	Approach
		Activities
		Adventure
Coxswain's Badge	–	Exercise
		Efficiency
		Expedition

Considered in a progressive and practical manner, the subheadings speak for themselves. They are in fact phased to accord development per boy age with activity leading to progressive efficiency. Sea Scouting must always be fun and provide action for the boy and this is why the intermediate stages to the badges are probably the most important. They are intended to create a programme over a period in themselves. Your basic sea activities programme should in fact be built around the respective "practice," "activities" and "efficiency" aspects of the three badges. They are the pivots of the whole plan.

A boy's particular talent to manage a boat or canoe can be easily spotted. It may even be sufficient for him to pass test for test — but such talent requires cultivation over a period to attain balanced efficiency. Experience will then also become a major part of the boy's progress. However, his interest must be maintained at a high pitch and towards this you will be required to provide a lively and varied programme of activities.

The ability to give service must be the ultimate aim for every Scout — and what better service can there be for a Sea Scout than to be able to effect rescue service afloat! This is why the sea training scheme embodies a surface-rescue element within the conditions of each of the three badges.

THE BOATMAN'S BADGE PROGRAMME

Training and water activities leading to this badge should be commenced with the award of the Scout Badge. The programme of training is designed to cover a period of approximately 18 months, which will mean that a boy joining from the Pack should normally complete the badge requirements by, say, 12½ years of age.

The object must be to provide a sound background for further activities afloat: to train the boy to manage a small craft under oars single-handed, in fair weather and water conditions; to become a useful member of a boat's crew under oars. Collectively, work for the badge should be used to develop the Patrol System afloat.

"Preparation" Stage

The importance of the boy learning to swim whilst in the Pack cannot be over emphasised. If he has not done so, passing the standard test as soon as possible after coming up into the Troop must be his first aim.

Generally the whole of this stage with the exception of swimming can be tackled by means of yarns and demonstrations. Every effort should be made, nevertheless, to make the training realistic and practical. Films and visual aids are most helpful, but an actual boat for demonstration purposes is a 'must.' The 'blackboard' approach to teaching seamanship should be dispensed with whenever possible.

"Practice" Stage

The first section of this stage has been deliberately introduced here and left out of the "preparation" stage in order to encourage Leaders to employ a practical approach in teaching a boy to use ropes. Demonstrate and practice on shore to begin with by all means, but arranging the requirements of the first section with the carefully planned activities of the second section must be the objective. The old broken spar, the Scout staff, or the kitchen chair leg is no substitute in a boy's mind for the actual thwart of a boat when the stress of the cable is evident.

This whole stage does in fact provide a framework on which to organise a pattern of Patrol boating activity afloat whether the stage be set for boat handling competitions, games for boats in company, or mock rescue exercises. The activities are also framed to provide older boys holding Coxswain's Mate badges (and candidates for this badge) with experience in taking charge of crews, development of leadership by demonstration in front of their Patrols, etc. All these activities should be undertaken on local boating water with variations suited to the local conditions.

"Project" Stage

The ultimate aim is now to bring all the varied aspects of the two earlier stages to function in the form of an interesting and enjoyable half-day feature afloat. This project must be adapted to local waters, boats and conditions — but should be planned to introduce the realism of a simple but effective surface rescue and salvage exercise. A sense of urgency compatible with efficiency and safety should be introduced by including flares and rockets if appropriate — discretion must, of course, remain with the Leader or Instructor.

A suggested outline programme for candidates is set out below, but should be treated as flexible to requirements. For instance, a measure of elementary signalling can be included if desired:

Complete a half-day's exercise, which must include —

The management under oars of a dinghy or similar single-handed craft, anchoring the craft, getting into the water and swimming ashore (or to an attendant craft).

Returning to the dinghy, rowing as bowman in a larger craft, getting aboard and lifting anchor, accepting a tow by heaving a line.

Casting off the tow, rowing to the shore, bringing the boat alongside and making fast.

Answering an emergency call to rescue, manning the dinghy, getting under way, rowing to a person in the water, assisting him aboard, and returning to the shore by sculling-over-the-stern.

Every effort should also be made to enlarge on the activities within the "practice" stage by arranging sailing parties to include these younger boys in crews and to encourage some canoeing activities.

During activities afloat every opportunity should also be used to put into practice a boy's Scoutcraft, with particular reference to local knowledge and first-aid.

THE COXSWAIN'S MATE BADGE PROGRAMME

The boy holding this badge can be accepted as being a thoroughly competent all-round member of a boat's crew, able to act as a pulling coxswain and take the helm under sail in normal weather conditions. He should be capable of taking a leading part in all water activities including a rescue service afloat.

The "activities" stage should be organised to cover a period of at least 18 months for 12/13-year-olds and be completed immediately after attaining 14 years of age.

The "Approach" Stage

This stage alone provides ample scope for the planning of an interesting and practical series of instructional talks, demonstrations and tests in observation both ashore and afloat. Every opportunity should be taken to arrange visits to Coastguard Stations, vessels in harbour, weather stations, lighthouses, boat-building yards and rigging establishments, etc. Small parties more often are far better from an instructional angle and indeed more welcome to the authority concerned, than large parties arranged at infrequent intervals.

As an additional subject for instruction ashore some chart work should be included, but this should be combined with some elementary compass work afloat.

The "Activities" Stage

The individual requirements at this stage speak for themselves. All boys should be encouraged, indeed trained, to take a part in maintaining the boats and equipment. As the boy progresses in the Troop he will automatically accept this task which will "spread the load" of annual maintenance, rather than this job falling on the shoulders of a few.

This is in fact probably the most important and interesting stage of the whole Sea Training Programme. It provides far-reaching scope for development. Activities should be staged on a Patrol basis to include younger and older boys and again can be embodied in boat handling evolutions, regattas and, most important of all— expeditions afloat under supervision.

The surface rescue element (Number 9) has been included at this stage to ensure that this form of training, leading to ability to give service, will figure regularly in the normal activities of the Troop.

As with the Boatman badge "Project," the actual test should be "rigged" to be as realistic as possible. A sense of urgency should be introduced — preparing the boy with the appropriate gear — getting under way (including a lifeboat style of launch if practicable) — the use of a jury rig sail in recovering the "stranded" craft if necessary. Boatman badge candidates should, of course, take part in this exercise also. The opportunity to gain experience of taking charge of them will be valuable to Patrol Leaders.

The "Adventure" Stage

This short expedition should be organised to combine as many aspects as possible from the earlier stages and should at the same time be closely associated with the parallel Scoutcraft requirements. Local waters should be utilised for this expedition whenever possible in order to give the boy the opportunity of extending his local knowledge of the area, tidal conditions, etc. Where journeys through commercial waterways are necessary, the presence of a Coastal Leader or Instructor as observer is quite in order; ideally he should be in a separate craft. Wherever possible, however, opportunity should be given to older boys holding the Coswain's badge to lead such expeditions.

A distance out of between 6 to 10 miles is sufficient for these expeditions, but a destination further afield will obviously add adventure and interest on inland waterways and smaller rivers.

To provide an even broader field of activity to this period of training, arrangements should be made for instruction in the management of outboard or inboard power craft, including the relevant safety precautions. A short canoeing expedition in company with other canoeists will provide added interest and variety, including a night in camp where practicable.

The development of canoe expeditions in company should in fact be given priority in some Groups at this stage. It is an ideal foil to the main programme of watermanship technique. Some Groups will be better situated for boat expeditions than others, but canoeing can be utilised in many circumstances as an alternative. A canoe, properly fitted for buoyancy and correctly stowed with provisions and equipment, will give a boy the chance of personal achievement from a journey that he could not perhaps undertake by boat because of confined and shallow waters. We should not forget, either, the advantage that a canoe enjoys when an obstruction appears ahead. The canoe can be lifted out of the water and carried around!

THE COXSWAIN'S BADGE PROGRAMME

This badge should occupy the older boy for approximately a year to eighteen months. Opportunity should be afforded to the more capable boy to complete the training as soon as possible in order that his skill as a Coxswain under oars and sail can be used to the full in instructing his Patrol. This is an important factor in the design of the general sea training scheme. You should in fact plan ahead, so that, by selective training, the Troop always has a proportion of boys in this category of efficiency. The full development of the Patrol System afloat should eventually result in this measure of efficiency being attained by the Patrol Leaders.

The "exercise" stage needs little explanation and should be "stepped up" in instructional intensity. If special short course classes can be organised there is no reason why Coxswain's Mate badge candidates should not also be allowed to participate. Care should be taken, however, not to make such classes too large in relation to the instructional facilities available.

The "efficiency" stage is again the main basis on which the water activities should be arranged. Number 4 should again be used to bring the younger boys into a more advanced form of rescue. Again, it must be made realistic and should be extended in area of operation with other incidents added to inspire quick thinking and ability to take charge afloat. For instance, emergency exercises such as Number 8 should be included whenever possible.

The "expedition" will be the highlight of the badge activities and should be given careful thought in the planning stages.

A positive aim should be given to the expedition and as many aspects of earlier training both ashore and afloat, particularly Scoutcraft, should be incorporated.

This expedition should be a regular feature in the programme — not merely an annual event — in order to give Coxswain's Mate candidates experience as crew members. *If local conditions are such that it is desirable that one or more adults accompany the expedition as emergency advisers and observers*, then this should be allowed for, but wherever practicable they should escort the expedition in another craft.

Note: In certain localities, e.g. estuaries subject to strong tidal surges, areas affected by unusual weather conditions or the like, it may be desirable to obtain a ruling on adult participation in journeys from the District Commissioner, who will be advised by his Sea Activities Committee.

Experience in charge of power craft should, whenever possible, be provided during the "efficiency" stages and elementary navigation ashore and afloat should be combined with the use of power craft.

To summarise the whole sea activities scheme, every opportunity should be taken to plan activities with a real purpose by incorporating individual skill, Patrol activity and inter-Troop competitions in the form of regattas and boat-handling displays. It is, in fact, a feature of the scheme to encourage Sea Scouts to display their skill in watermanship more to the general public.

A separate chapter has not been allotted to programme planning simply because it is not considered necessary. The three-badge Sea Training scheme provides ample material within its progressive requirements on which to build a balanced programme. Nonetheless, planning ahead is absolutely essential. In close liaison with the Patrol Leaders' Council, the application of the proposed sea activities badge programme should be mapped out months ahead. This is the only way of meeting all the varied activities envisaged.

The detailed programme of such activities should be displayed prominently in the Headquarters. The modern boy has many commitments, both in and out of the school curriculum —he has often other interests besides Scouting — *but*, experience has proved that if a boy can visualise a plan of his future Scouting, he will be anxious to participate with ambition to succeed.

There is no disguising the fact that a major reason for poor attendance at Scout activities is often that boys are not informed until the night before! This is no good for the modern boy — *he has usually made other arrangements*!

EXTENDED SEA TRAINING PROGRAMMES

Provision must be made for the boy who has an obvious talent or natural bent towards more specialised activities. For instance, during the later stages of the Coxswain's Mate badge programme, evidence may be seen of some boys showing particular interest in the more advanced proficiency badges. This desire should be encouraged even if it requires 'harnessing' in relation to available facilities and the physical capabilities of the boy. His skill in a particular field will, with careful instruction and experience, prove useful to you and the other Leaders and Instructors. This development can be channelled into any of the following proficiency badge activities:

Pursuit Badges:

Boatswain – needs no explanation as to usefulness.

Canoeist – includes construction and maintenance, and to develop Scoutcraft journey by water.

Communicator – includes visual and W/T signals.

Mechanic – as applied to marine I.C.E. and diesel engines.

Meteorologist – as applied to local weather conditions.

Power Coxswain – intended to be the most progressive lead to taking charge afloat and an excellent preparation for future sea activities.

Race Helmsman – to develop racing techniques and a positive lead to competitive Sea Scouting afloat plus further preparation for Venture sea activities.

Service Badges

Lifesaver – needs no explanation as to usefulness.

Pilot – should, where possible, be *gradually* developed as part of Coxswain's badge early stage training, with alternatives to suit; and be usefully applied to all local waters.

The requirements of these badges have been designed to make them forceful in approach and flexible in relation to local conditions, in order to employ the skills acquired in a truly operational sense.

The long-term value of the Instructor range of proficiency badges cannot be over-emphasised. Great use can be found for the older boy with sound and balanced experience obtained from the Sea Training Programme and the capability to instruct in watermanship and the allied skills afloat.

Extended activities in liaison with other Youth Organisations and Sailing, Rowing and Canoeing Clubs will be more easily attainable if the full field of activities afloat is progressively planned for and incorporated in the training of the Troop.

ROYAL NAVAL RECOGNITION

Sea Scout Troops who attain a certain high standard in numbers and training may apply to take part in the Royal Navy Recognition Scheme. If an initial Inspection by an Officer of the Royal Navy proves successful, Royal Navy Recognition is granted; then special badges may be worn and an R.N. Recognition Pennant flown by the Troop. Special privileges, including visits to R.N. ships, are given to Recognised Troops by the Royal Navy.

Full details and application forms are available from the Programme and Training Department at Headquarters.

SAFETY STANDARDS

From the wide field of activities described must inevitably come the problem of maintaining safety with activity. Ability to swim and stay afloat is the first requirement, but refusal to take unjustified risks is the foremost consideration for every Scout Leader and Instructor.

All three "Sea" badges demand a positive approach to efficiency afloat, which in itself contributes to safety afloat — both individually and collectively. Nevertheless, the safety rules of boating must be tactfully repeated in all activities right from the start so that their observation becomes instinctive. Every boy should also be made familiar with local boating rules as part of his upbringing. Remember, the honest but intelligent observation of the few necessary rules will avoid the gradual introduction of more restrictive ones. Local Harbour regulations are made for a good reason and Scouts afloat should set an example in conforming with them.

To this end many of the activities that can be organised around the Sea Training Programme should include emergency exercises related to local conditions and hazards.

Charge Certificates will apply in various categories to the many different types of water. They must be constantly reviewed in relation to a boy's capabilities, the need for encouragement being tempered with considerations of safety. No difficulty need arise, however, if limitations are lifted concurrently with progress made in the Sea Training Programme *on or about the Troop's normal boating waters*. Experience must be looked upon as the best evidence of fitness for extending the field of operation covered by the Certificate. The subject of reviewing boys' Charge Certificates should be a regular item on the agenda of the Group Scouters' Meeting. In the case of the more extended area Class "B" Charge Certificates for boys and Class "A" and "B" for Leaders and Instructors, constant review by the local Sea Activities Committee is an important aspect of their terms of reference.

FACILITIES AND EQUIPMENT

This chapter is not intended to tell you how to get the necessary craft, equipment and allied facilities. It is rather in the nature of general guidance on the types of boat and facilities considered best suited to sea activities for Scouts. The Programme and Training Department at Headquarters will from time to time issue advice on how to obtain specific boats and equipment, or will advise in response to applications from Groups or Sea Activities Committees.

(a) Choice of Water and Location of Courses

The principle to remember with regard to facilities is "home waters are best in the long run." Avoid having to travel as much as possible when thinking in terms of basic training afloat. Time spent getting across country is time afloat missed. A boy wants to do his Sea Scouting on his own doorstep as much as possible — and in boats belonging to his own Group. There is no substitute for this.

A central training ground and water in a County or area is good for special activities, regattas, courses, etc., but the number of hours available per boy per craft under such arrangements is very limited. It also means that a boy must go to his parents for his fare, etc., every time the Troop goes afloat. This is something Leaders will wish to avoid. The establishment and development of activities, including courses, on as local a basis as possible should be your aim.

(b) Boats

Unless a Group has a fleet of small boats, pulling and/or sailing, too many younger boys will spend far too much time on shore 'waiting their turn' and watching others. The basic means of training young coxswains must be available. Two main types of boat are essential for the general training of Sea Scouts, one (a) able to carry a crew of five or more, and the other (b) capable of being managed single-handed.

Of (a), the most generally useful type is the four- or six-oared coxed gig, of which there are many classes. Such boats afford means of training in:

(i) Patrol activities
(ii) Boat discipline and crew work
(iii) Taking charge
(iv) Expeditions.

Older classes include Longridge, Old Thames, Thames and Coastguard gigs. A modern, but expensive, class is the 20-ft.

"Home Counties" fibreglass gig, suitable for use on inland and more sheltered coastal waters.

Particulars of these boats and of others suitable for use in more exposed waters can be obtained from the Programme and Training Department.

Ex-naval and similar whalers and cutters are in use by some established Groups and have the advantage of being cheap when they can be obtained. They are now little used by the Royal Navy and are, therefore, difficult to come by. The whaler and, even more so, the cutter are too heavy and unhandy for younger boys under oars, but they are very sturdily built and have their uses as sailing craft in more open waters, the whaler particularly being a fine sea-boat, suitable for cruises and expeditions along the coast.

(b) The second category presents less of a problem because there are many suitable dinghies on the market and their cost is so much less. The 'Sea Scout,' fibreglass, 11ft. 6in., pulling and sailing, is a good example of a reliable general-purpose boat in this category.

The provision of 'class' sailing dinghies for older boys is important with the introduction of the Race Helmsman proficiency badge. There are so many class boats to select from that it is not within the compass of this supplement to say one is more suitable than another.

In coastal areas with local craft adapted to local conditions, it is to be expected that these types will find favour also with local Groups. Whatever type of craft is being considered, however, local building should always be considered if the drawn line plans of the boat are available. Experience has shown that the local boat-builder's quotation often proves the cheapest in the long run.

TECHNICAL TRAINING FOR LEADERS

Briefly there are four methods of imparting technical training to Leaders and prospective Leaders in sea activities for Scouts:

(a) on a National basis – by courses at an Activity Centre.
(b) On a Regional, County or Area basis, by courses arranged at a suitable centre of activity.
(c) on local waters by courses of progressive instruction

organised by local Sea Activities Committees.

(d) by experience, from boy and youth to adult, of a comprehensive scheme of sea training through the Group — plus recognised leadership courses.

The last, (d), is likely to be the soundest, but unfortunately is not applicable to all. The most practicable for the newcomer to Scouting is (c). It will be spread over a period and, therefore, will be a means of gaining experience in itself. It is also likely to be carried out in the craft and on the waters on which your boys will operate. Both methods will be supplemented by (a) and (b), particularly in specialist fields. Training in the more advanced sea activities will probably only be available through (a) or (b).

Amongst the training opportunities must be included recognised courses and activities sponsored and arranged by other Organisations such as The Sports Council, the British Canoe Union, the Youth Service, etc. Their different approach to the task will be welcome, whether it be by way of equipment used, methods applied or the syllabus itself. Not only the technical knowledge obtainable from such courses should be considered. Ideas, methods of instructing and aids to organising activities are the principal features to be absorbed from such courses — in other words, how to pass on knowledge to the modern boy, which is the vital factor to be considered.

Your local Sea Activities Committee or Activities Adviser should have information about such opportunities, but if not, details will be available on application to the Headquarters of the Organisations concerned.

Chapter 25

AIR SCOUT SUPPLEMENT

ADVENTURE IN THE AIR FOR ALL SCOUTS

There is air all around us; it is with us all our days, in the park or in the Troop room; it is with us winter and summer; it is absolutely free; it is our very breath of life, and yet it has, and always will, hold a promise of adventure for the man who seeks to master it. Although so necessary to our existence, the air generally remains untouched and unexplored by the majority of us, but for those who dare to venture beyond the earth's surface it promises untold adventures and excitements. Scouting is an adventure and the air can add a new dimension to your programme.

You don't need to be an Air Scout or an expert to explore the air around you. Most air activities can be tackled with few items of equipment and simple common sense. The variety is almost endless and is increasing every day with new inventions and developments in aviation. They can add flavour to your programme, indoors or out.

USING THE AIR IN SCOUTING

We must never forget the aim of our Scout Movement nor the method by which we seek to achieve our aim. Thus an air activity should never merely be an end in itself. Don't be tempted to involve your Scouts in some dull and tedious labour merely because it has a remote connection with the air. Air activities should be well conceived with an aim in view which every boy can understand. It should involve something practical and not just "pretending." It should involve something new and exciting and not merely be a re-hash of some old outmoded game to give it an "air bias."

For example, why not choose an air activity to show Scouts that air can exert a force, and that it can influence other Scouting activities such as sailing and rock climbing. Start off with a simple kite, learn how to fly it and why it flies. Measure the force on the kite string under various wind conditions and with the kite at various heights, showing that the force alters with the wind speed and that the wind speed alters with height. Explain why this happens and show what happens to the kite in gusty conditions or in the lee of a house or tree. It is now hardly necessary to illustrate how wind can affect a boat sailing on a narrow lake between high mountains or a Scout climbing a high rock face. If you do not know all the answers yourself there are many books available to help you.

The range of air activities is endless. At the end of this chapter you will find a list of some of them, but you can also find them in SCOUTING and in other Scout publications. You will be able to glean them from various Flying Organisations and Model Clubs. You may get ideas from aviation magazines or from other Scout Leaders, but best of all think up your own ideas. In the end it gives you the most satisfaction and the Scouts the most fun.

SAFETY FIRST

Every airfield belongs to someone. It may look empty or disused for the time being but there is no way of knowing when an aircraft may appear from nowhere, or a glider is towed into the sky or a parachutist falls from above. Even a single Scout standing where he should not be may cause a serious accident either to himself or to the user of the airfield. You are reminded of the *P.O.R.* regulations regarding Access to Airfields. The best plan is to obtain permission before setting out for your airfield, but if you are on an expedition and you come across an interesting airfield, you must get permission before entering or crossing. Remember that many of our air activities take place on airfields and with the assistance of our aviation contacts. If you disregard these instructions you may alienate these friends from the Scout Movement and completely queer the pitch for yourself, as well as for those who come after you.

Flying in an aircraft and "having a go" at the controls can be great fun. However, you are reminded of the *P.O.R.* regulations on flying.

You will depend for most of your flying and air experience on the goodwill of other people. The more you assist them by ensuring your Scouts are prepared for the flight, the more likely you are to be offered subsequent flights.

For many years it has been the proud boast of the Scout Movement that they make do and mend wherever possible. In air activities this rule does not hold good. Remember that when someone or something drops from the sky, damage invariably is the result. In all your air activities use equipment in new and good condition and *never* take unnecessary risks.

The most important rule of all is left entirely to you. Use your common sense and don't take a chance.

THE AIR TRAINING PROGRAMME

Air activities are open to all Scouts, but there are some who will wish to become specialists and tackle more adventurous air activities. These will form a generation of air experts to try out new activities and to pass them on to others. As more enterprising activities are tackled the degree of knowledge and skill must increase. So for the Scout who shows more than a passing interest in the air there is offered a logical and progressive training. This is called the Air Training Programme. It is supplementary to the Scout Training Scheme and each of the three stages are awarded only after the Scouting skills have been mastered. The Airman's Badge can be started immediately after enrolment but cannot be awarded until the Scout Standard has been gained. Similarly, the Senior Airman's Badge can be started though not awarded until the Advance Scout Standard has been gained. The Master Airman's Badge may be awarded at any time after this. Scouts who attain the various stages of the Air Training Programme have a standard which is easily recognisable by all members of the Movement as well as by members of the aviation world.

Air Scouts will be expected to follow the air training programme as a matter of course rather than of choice, the aim being to prepare the Scout for what must be the ultimate goal of almost every air-minded youth, namely, to fly an aircraft on his own. It follows closely the pattern of training offered in other flying Organisations while still maintaining the characteristic methods of the Scout Movement. Many Scouts may not reach the goal of being able to fly on their own but will still benefit from the training and from the experience gained.

The training detailed in the programme comes under three distinct sections: flight safety and airmanship, aviation knowledge and practical experience, and follows a progressive and related pattern. As the Scout absorbs the knowledge offered in the various badges he fits himself for more exciting and adventurous air activities. For example, a Scout who possesses the Airman's Badge can be expected to visit an airfield with only the slightest supervision. A Scout who possesses his Senior Airman's Badge should be able to render valuable assistance to aviators in and around the airfield besides being able to take part in air experience flights in dual-controlled aircraft. The Scout who possesses the Master Airman's Badge should be able to undertake a course of flying instruction, with much of the ground work and some of the air work having been already covered.

In some of the tests in the Air Training Programme, alternatives are given to allow the Scout to follow his own particular interest in aviation. There is no need for him to choose the same alternative subject in subsequent badges.

The notes on the Air Training Programme which follow must be read in conjunction with the details published in *P.O.R.* and are only a guide to assist you organise your training.

The Airman's Badge

It is not always possible to meet on or near an airfield and much of the Air Training Programme might appear to be of a theoretical nature. But the Scout method is not to teach by lectures or lessons but by games and practical experiments. So whether the subject is the layout of an airfield or the parts of an aircraft, use either the real thing or models.

When dealing with *P.O.R.* "Access to Airfields" you should choose the airfield you visit most frequently, but don't forget that if you visit another airfield you must obtain another briefing to comply with the rules.

Moving on to parts of an aircraft, don't be tempted to ask for too many parts of an aircraft. The air-minded Scout will know these soon enough. But for his own safety and for his better understanding of air activities he should know the basics such as: fuselage, main plane, tail plane, fin, ailerons, elevators, rudder, leading and trailing edges, undercarriage, engine nacelle, intake, exhaust, propellor.

When dealing with the first practical test, the trimming of a glider, you must make the glider yourself. It should be a simple stick fuselage with 1/16″ balsa wings suitably sanded and of not more than 12″ span. There should be 3/4″ dihedral and 1/16″ incidence. Weight the nose with plasticine until the model balances while supported 1/3 of the way back from the leading edge at the wing tips. You will find it is quite simple, but make several in case of breakage. Of course, first experiment yourself to make sure that you can make the glider do all that is required of it. As the Scout alters the trim of the glider you have a marvellous opportunity for introducing some of the basic principles of flight. Remember the practical test must be effective. If it is not, send the Scout away to practise on his own under the guidance of his Patrol Leader.

Senior Airman's Badge

All Scouts should be instructed at this stage in strapping on and use of the Royal Air Force pattern seat parachute and in the necessity for, and use of, aircraft safety harness. But don't forget that in some aircraft you may find different equipment which will in turn involve a fresh briefing.

As air experience flights are still comparatively rare, there is an unfortunate tendency to try and cram as much as possible into a short flight. For the uninitiated Scout there is adventure enough in finding himself airborne without being subjected to an aerobatic display, close formation flying, followed by a low level beat-up of the airfield. He is likely to be permanently discouraged by this exhibition. The first air experience flight should be a simple and short affair and should include little more than gentle turns and a "feel" of the controls. Later on he can be introduced to more violent manoeuvres as long as he is told beforehand what to expect.

The type of safety equipment used in the aircraft in which you obtain most of your flying will determine whether you cover tumbling and the use of the parachute, or the life-saving jacket. Many civilian aircraft operating near or over the sea will have only the life-saving jackets, while all the light service aircraft use the parachute.

Master Airman's Badge

The Scout will have decided by this time whether he wishes to continue with a course of flying instruction or, while still interested in aviation, he would rather remain with his feet firmly on the ground. If he chooses the latter course he should be encouraged to tackle some practical type of research. All other Scouts should be encouraged and prepared to take some form of flying course, either on gliders or powered aircraft. No-one is able to fly solo under Ministry of Aviation Rules until he reaches the age of 17.

Scout Wings

Although the Air Training Programme, as such, finishes within the Scout section, Venture Air Scouts and air-minded Venture Scouts may wish to avail themselves of the many flying instruction courses available. Thus the ultimate goal of being able to fly solo must be left to the Venture Scout section.

AIR SCOUTING

Although all Scouts are able to take part in air activities and may follow the Air Training Programme at any stage, there will be some whose interests in the air and aviation are so great that they will wish to follow the Air Training Programme, as well as concentrating on air activities, throughout their days in the Scout Movement. A Scout in this category should be encouraged to join a specialist Air Scout Troop rather than any other, and if this aviation interest develops after joining another Troop he should be encouraged and advised, where practical, to transfer to an Air Scout Troop. If there are several Scouts in your Troop who share a common interest in aviation, then you may consider forming an Air Scout Patrol. But whether they are Air Scout Patrols or Troops, they are first and foremost Scouts, take the same Promise,

adhere to the same Law and follow the same basic training, but wherever possible they look to the air for their activities and adventure.

Because the Air Scout Troop follows so actively a pattern of air training they can very often engage in even more exciting air activities than members of the other branches and can often gain access into aviation circles which other Scouts would be denied. They should be easily distinguished as air specialists by the public at large so the uniform is orientated towards the Airlines and Air Forces.

Air Scouts, with their interest in aviation and their solid background of air training, can render invaluable service in many different ways, from assisting in the local flying club to acting as officials at large air displays. But more important than service outside the Movement is the service that Air Scout Troops can render to their fellow Scouts by providing a qualified and experienced crew to guide and assist in air activities within the District or County. Their Leaders should form the nucleus of the Movement's gliding Instructors, while the Venture Air Scouts might become Instructors in any air activity from parascending to hot air ballooning. Air Advisers at District or County level should always be available to assist and advise any Scouts in their air activities.

THE AIR SCOUT LEADER

The Air Scout Leader is first and foremost a Scout Leader. Even more than that, he should be a *good* Scout Leader, as running an Air Scout Troop can be even more demanding than running an ordinary Troop. If you really feel that you cannot master the air training and can only tackle the straightforward Scouting side, then you must ensure that you have adequate Instructors and Assistants to be able to put over the Air Training Programme. Even if you do feel you can teach the aeronautical as well as the Scouting side you should try to collect around you a team of specialists and Instructors who can relieve you of much of the more advanced air training and can think up new and exciting ways of teaching the air subjects.

Having decided that you can do it yourself, or having obtained the assistance of an expert, don't fall into the trap of using the "lecture technique" to teach your air subjects. This smacks of the classroom and school and most Scouts will have had sufficient of that during the day without continuing in the evening. Wherever you can, use the Scout methods of getting information across, by games, demonstrations, building models, doing or seeing the real thing. Your job as the Scout Leader must be to decide what information is required from the expert and then to "get it across" in the most attractive way possible.

There are many other ways of getting aviation information across to your Scouts. There are excellent films, both cartoon and documentary, available from many sources, and which cover the basic principles of flight as well as a large number of allied subjects. A judicious use of film strips or slides can be of great assistance, especially if you make your own. Charts and diagrams on the wall offer an almost unconscious method of teaching and can also add a touch of colour to the Troop Room. But best of all, try and make your air instruction practical. Get out onto an airfield, work with aircraft, see them and touch them, and if this is impossible then design, build and fly your own models or conduct simple wind tunnel experiments with an old vacuum cleaner.

Making good contacts and obtaining assistance is probably one of the most important tasks of the Air Scout Leader. The Movement can never provide all the air experience and gliding to satisfy the demand from Scouts, so a great deal of it will have to be obtained from outside Bodies. Besides that, many of your activities in the Air Scout Troop, as well as Instructors, will come from, or be sponsored by, outside Bodies; therefore good relations are essential. In all these contacts it is not just a case of what we can get out, but also what we can put back in, in the form of service and assistance, good turns and the sharing of knowledge. Here is a list of some of the Bodies where you might get assistance in your Air Scouting: The Royal Air Force, the Air Training Corps, the Royal Observer Corps, the Fleet Air Arm, Gliding Clubs, Flying Clubs, Parachuting Clubs, Aeromodelling Clubs, the Private Pilots' Association, the Aviation Industry, Civil Airlines. In the case of the Service Organisations, always write first to the Officer Commanding and he will ensure that it is passed to the person who can offer you the most assistance. Don't try and call on your first contact. When dealing with the Clubs and Private Pilots' Associations, write first to the Secretary requesting an interview. Most Secretaries of Clubs are voluntary posts and they are invariably very busy people with time at an absolute premium. When dealing with the Aviation Industry or Civilian Airlines, always write first to the Public Relations Officer who will then put you in touch with the department which can offer you the most help. All these outside Organisations deal mainly with professionals and it is, therefore, up to the Air Scout Leader to be "professional" in his dealings with them. Courtesy, promptness and the typewritten letters are a good starting point. Offers of service, enthusiasm, spontaneous pleasure, and letters of thanks, will always make it easier the second time. On every occasion show that you are proud to be a member of the Movement and that you appreciate the responsibility involved in running a Troop and introducing the Scouts to the world of aviation.

If we give the right impression as Air Scout Leaders to all those, both inside and outside the Movement, with whom we come in contact, we will not only encourage a better understanding of the branch but will also attract offers of assistance, which are so important in providing an exciting and adventurous Air Training Programme.

THE R.A.F. RECOGNITION SCHEME

Air Scout Troops who reach a certain standard in numbers and training may take part in the R.A.F. Recognition Scheme. This involves an inspection by a person appointed by the Royal Air Force which, if successful, results in the granting of Royal Air Force recognition to the Air Scout Troop. This honour carries with it some extra privileges from the Royal Air Force, and in order to retain Royal Air Force recognition, the Air Scout Troop must pass the inspection each year. At any stage, however, they can elect to leave the Scheme and remain Air Scouts.

PROGRAMME PLANNING

In all your programme planning the basic Scouting skills come first and the standard must be high. As an Air Scout Leader you should aim to use air activities wherever you can to assist you in the Scout training. When planning your Scouting programme, it is also advisable to plan a parallel programme of air activities both long and short term. Many of the more exciting air activities take some time to prepare and invariably they will require some form of equipment and specialist instruction. The large number of courses available for gliding and flying also come into the category of long term planning. However, before making any firm bookings you are recommended to seek advice from your Activities Adviser or, failing that, direct from the Air Training Centre, Lasham Airfield, Nr. Alton, Hants, in order to ensure that the course you have chosen is of an acceptable standard to satisfy both our own experts and our Insurance Company. Do not be discouraged by the cost involved for these courses, as there are many forms of grant to cover either the whole of a course or part of it.

AIR ACTIVITIES AND PROJECTS

There are many air activities and projects which can be tackled by Scouts. Some require costly equipment and specialist supervision and will be organised on a National or Regional level. Others, less demanding, will be available at County or District level. Many more will be undertaken at Group level.

The following is a recommended list of air activities.

1. Suitable for organising on a National or County level.

Gliding
Powered Flying
Parachuting
Parascending
Primary Glider Training
Practical Navigation
Gyro-Gliding
Hovercraft building and flying.

2. Suitable for organising at Troop or Patrol level.

All types of model aircraft and hovercraft construction.
Model flying, including control line, whip line and radio control.
Kite building and flying. Suggested types: competition, weight lifting, high flying, and fighting.
Building and using a simple cockpit trainer.
Wind tunnel experiments using an old vacuum cleaner.
Building and maintaining a Troop weather station.
Aircraft recognition and spotting.

Satellite model building and satellite spotting.
Two minute and paper model building and flying
Building a Troop hovercraft.
Model hot air balloon building and flying.

Chapter 26

TRAINING AIDS

How often has one of your Scouts muffled a yawn, another cleared his throat rather obviously, and a third talked to a fourth while you have been giving a talk? "I know it's asking rather a lot to expect you to keep still for half an hour," you sigh in desperation, "but hang on for just a few minutes longer and I'll be finished." If you have experienced this situation, there has been a failure in communication somewhere. Many have the gift of the gab, few have mastered the art of public speaking; many are able lecturers, few are born teachers.

The advertisements in glossy magazines, newspapers and on TV might goad you to go to work on an egg, but you are likely to use a more convenient means of transport. In this and a host of other examples which could be cited, you take advantage of the facilities available. And "take advantage" *is* the correct phrase in this context, for it means to "avail oneself of circumstance" and *not* to exploit or over-reach an individual whom you have caught at a *dis*advantage.

Fifty years ago, few realised that the world was on the verge of a technological revolution, a revolution which would be more profound and far-reaching than the industrial one which preceded it a century before. In the last two decades this revolution has gathered momentum, and its direct and indirect effects have touched almost every fibre of society, perhaps none more pre-eminently than communication.

TRAINING AIDS

Communication is not a gimmick but an integral part of the age in which we live, and in the field of transmitting knowledge and ideas to young people *effective* communication has become of increasing importance. Effective communication requires — purpose, efficiency, vitality, and intelligibility. These four basic attributes should be present whatever the *means* of communication employed. Children no longer have their education 'drummed into them.' A wind of change, blowing away the chalk dust, is sweeping through many classrooms, and children no longer find their education the unavoidable imposition of an adult world, but an exciting experience. Television, newspapers, magazines and a host of other media have made a dramatic impact. Young people have the world in their sights at the press of a switch; they can see what is happening on the other side of the world *as it happens*. They thirst for information, and, having been born in an era of change, they are used to — and expect — things to change and to be on the move. Education, training, or whatever you like to call it, in schools, youth clubs and elsewhere, today develops *all* a child's latent potential by making him a participator *as well as* an observer.

Scouting gives a boy a training, the opportunity to become an individual, *and* something more. Many Organisations have tried to emulate Scouting but none has succeeded. There *is* a Scouting "magic": it's an inexplicable, indefinable quality which appeals to boys the world over. The "magic" is companionship, enterprise, imagination, responsibility, achievement. However, to a greater or lesser extent, the amount of the "magic" is related to the soundness of the training. If the training is not assimilated or only partially effective for whatever reason — the inadequacy of the Leader or the inattention or misunderstanding of the boy — then the foundations will be insecure and so affect the boy's Scouting as a whole. This is where training aids can be of real help.

Much of Scouting is orientated to outdoor activities and to practical pursuits. The Progress Scheme not only retains almost all the basic skills which always have been fundamental to Scouting, but extends the scope of activities — indoor and outdoor — which a boy can enjoy within the framework of his Scouting. No one man, however brilliant, can hope — or indeed is expected — to train, teach and examine the Scouts in his Troop in each of the wide range of subjects now open to them. Whether or not there had been an Advance Party in 1966 and a new Progress Scheme, there would still have been a need to radically review training techniques in many Troops. Often there is either too much theory and too little practice, or a minimum of theory resulting in the practice being far from perfect. Training and practice go together — the one complements the other.

The spirit or "magic" of Scouting will not be endangered by the adoption of new training techniques: they are, in fact, more likely to have a salutary effect. An Organisation which does not make maximum use of the available resources is in grave danger of alienating itself from those whom it exists to serve.

Boys detest a lecture unless it is delivered by an experienced public speaker, who has something of interest to say, *and* who expresses himself in a manner which attracts and retains their attention. Even so, half an hour (probably twenty minutes) is about as much as they can take before their interest wanes. But with even the simplest training aids boys can be held in rapt attention for some considerable time.

Having argued the case for the use of training aids, we can now discuss a selection of the aids available, how to use them, and where to get them.

1. POSTERS AND WALL CHARTS

(a) **"Home made"** — as their purpose is primarily to give information, usually of a forthcoming event, they should be:

bold to catch the eye and demand further attention;

informative to provide all the basic details (event, date, time, place, cost);

timely to give plenty of advance notice (some people do have other things to do); and

displayed properly in prominent places so that they can be seen (it's a rare bird that goes to look for a poster).

Immediately after the event they should be removed.

(b) **Others** — a useful means of 'static' communication to stimulate interest, to impart information, to proffer advice and to give directions (e.g. Accident Prevention, National Parks, Maps). *BUT* ring the changes. A tatty poster which has been hanging on the wall for months is useless. If new or different posters are displayed regularly, they will serve their purpose — communication: if they're left to gather dust they become no more than pieces of unusually designed wallpaper.

(c) **Wall Charts** — principal purpose to give information about a *subject*. Useful aid, provided they *are* used. Some are available free, others cost a few coppers. The importance of using wall charts cannot be overstressed. If they are changed regularly the boys *will* look at them. The old ones need not be thrown away, but can be put into the Troop library and brought out again at a later date.

(d) **General** — a theme for the month with wall charts *and* posters (e.g. travel, sailing, careers, the town, flying, the country, accidents, industry, agriculture, international sport, etc.).

2. NOTICEBOARDS

Where they exist they are often so overcrowded with so much so-called information that many do not bother to look at them. Keep essential notices neat and tidy and ruthlessly discard antiquated ones. Make the noticeboard large, and why not fix it on the *outside* wall of the Troop Headquarters or make a free-standing unit? A noticeboard which is locked away *inside* is of little use between meetings — and why shouldn't you tell those outside the Troop (parents, policemen on the beat, shoppers — all passers-by) what you're doing?

3. DISPLAYS

A variation on the "theme for a month" mentioned in Posters and Wall Charts, or for special events (e.g. A.G.M.s, training courses, camps) for "internal" consumption, or as a public relations aid for a Parents' Evening *or* for the Group Open Day when you have a golden opportunity to tell the public about Scouting in general and your Troop's achievements in particular.

4. MODELS

Much more effective than sketches of doubtful artistic merit. They are training aids and their design and construction provide worthwhile projects for the boys. (Layout of camp site, conservation, pioneering, topography, fire construction, air-fields, etc.).

5. FLIPBOARDS

A series of charts or drawings to illustrate a talk which helps to make even the most uninteresting subject come alive at Troop Headquarters or out in the open. The sheets of cartridge paper (about 20" x 25") have holes punched at the top to fit a ring binder. On each succeeding sheet, diagrams or sketches are drawn to illustrate the principal points of your talk — the "pages" are flipped over as you go along.

6. PHOTOGRAPHS

Unless incorporated in a display they are of limited value. In a training session they should be large enough to be seen *clearly* by those who are farthest away from the speaker. Can be a great asset in a small discussion group provided they are good.

7. TRANSPARENCIES

Invariably colour is more attractive than black and white. Wherever possible, divorce the speaker and the projectionist. The speaker should be at the front so that everyone can hear what he is saying, and the projectionist should be hidden unobtrusively in the shadows at the back.

Home made — It is inadvisable to show every slide in the box. Select only the best. If you are the "lecturer," prepare some notes on what you intend saying. Keep the show moving: far better the lads should wish you had left a slide on the screen a second or two longer than to lose their interest. Apart from the obvious subjects (camp, the regatta, the District and County competitions, etc.), sets of slides on such subjects as signs, trees at all seasons, competitions, etc., will have greater impact than Wall Charts alone, especially if they have been taken in the locality of the Troop Headquarters.

Others — Numerous Organisations have a free slide lending service (particularly overseas government tourist offices). Most provide notes for speakers (and some will provide the speaker as well) and supplementary visual material — brochures, leaflets, pamphlets.

8. FILM STRIPS

For training, interest or entertainment there is a greater scope in film strips for training aids than in slides. A principal source of film strips is the National Council for Audio-Visual Aids in Education (see P. 242/3). Filmstrips, once purchased, can also be cut up and made into slides.

9. FILMS

A selection of films (8mm. and 16mm.) on several subjects during the Winter months gives variety to Troop Meetings which might tend to drag during bad weather when outdoor activities are curtailed. Films — silent and sound, black and white and colour — are available on almost any subject on free loan, on the payment of handling costs, or at hire charges which range from 5/6d. upwards depending on age, length, sound, colour, etc. Films made by The Scout Association are available on hire from Guild Sound & Vision Ltd., Kingston Road, Merton Park, London, S.W.19.

10. RECORDINGS

If the Group has a tape recorder or can borrow one now and again there's considerable scope for the use of sound. However, it should be borne in mind that interest flags rapidly when people (young and old alike) are expected to do no more than sit and listen to a succession of sounds. However, the occasional 5 to 10 minutes recording of types of folk music, local dialects, industrial noises, etc., interspersed with explanatory commentary, can be interesting, especially if a group of your Scouts has made the recording.

11. OTHER AIDS

The audio-visual aids described (i.e. sound and sight) are not the only training techniques. There are also many ways in which the other three senses — touch, smell and taste — can be employed to put the ideas across.

For example — *Touch:* materials, minerals, ropes.
Smell: cheeses, woodsmoke, herbs, flowers.
Taste: beverages, fruits, fish.

These aids are not independent of one another. There will be many occasions on which, with careful planning and preparation, a subject can be put across requiring the Scouts to use three, four or all their senses.

Example: A Cookery Evening

Wall Charts and Posters displayed round Headquarters.
Film on tea, flour, meat, etc.
Tasting session — different blends of tea, coffee, etc.
Film strip — cocoa and chocolate production.
Smelling session — putting the name to a variety of cheese by its odour.
Trying a new recipe — demonstration.

Example: Summer Camp

Notice board — advance announcement of visits to site by Scout Leader and representatives of the Patrol Leaders' Council.
Display board — with maps and photographs of camp site, together with local guide book, references for obtaining further information.
Posters — to maintain interest — the first one put up should not still be hanging, faded and tattered, when you get back.
Slides and/or films of the site and surrounding area, local industries, etc.

Where to get a projector

(if the Group does not have one).

(a) Many Local Education Authorities will make projectors available on free loan, *provided* there is someone who has received instruction in projection, often on a course run by the Local Education Authority. It is sound policy to have two or three "qualified" projectionists in the Troop.

(b) Some Organisations which loan films will provide a projector, operator and speaker.

(c) There may be a local photographic shop whose proprietor will lend a projector gratis or for a nominal charge.

The National Organisation for Audio-Visual Aids

254/256 Belsize Road, London, N.W.6.

TRAINING AIDS

There are three sections in this Organisation, all of which were set up by the Ministry of Education, Local Education Authorities and Teachers' Organisations.

1. **The National Committee for Audio-Visual Aids in Education** is responsible for the formulation of national policy, the promotion of audio-visual methods and the provision of an information service on audio-visual matters. Of particular interest for Scout Leaders is The Visual Education National Information Service for Schools (VENISS) which provides a constant flow of information, much of which is useful in Scout training as well as in schools.

Among the reference sources published are:
The National Catalogue of Films and Filmstrips (published in eight sections).
Supplementary Catalogues and Lists including:
- United Nations filmstrips.
- UNESCO filmstrips.
- Granada zoological films.

Free lists of specialised films and filmstrips.
Catalogue of wall charts.
Supplementary visual material — listing more than 170 national and industrial sources of all types of audio-visual aids.

2. **The Education Foundation for Visual Aids** has special responsibility for the distribution, production and cataloguing of educational films and filmstrips, the supply of equipment and the provision of technical, advisory and maintenance services.

The Foundation's Film Library at Weybridge in Surrey holds for distribution a very wide range of 16mm. films and film loops, 35mm. filmstrips, and a number of 2" x 2" slides. Approximately 1,700 films and 4,000 filmstrips are available.

3. **National Visual Aids Centre** has three main departments —
(a) *Equipment and Technical Division* with an extensive permanent display of all types of audio-visual equipment, etc.
(b) *Experimental Development Unit* — for research.
(c) *Training Branch* which organises courses on specific audio-visual techniques.

INDEX

INDEX

INDEX

INDEX

INDEX

INDEX

INDEX